AMERICA'S FUTURE:

AN ISLAMIC SURGE, ISIS, AL QAEDA, WORLD EPIDEMICS, UKRAINE, RUSSIA-CHINA PACT, US LEADERSHIP CRISIS

STEPHEN BLAHA

AMERICA'S FUTURE:

AN ISLAMIC SURGE, ISIS, AL QAEDA, WORLD EPIDEMICS, UKRAINE, RUSSIA-CHINA PACT, US LEADERSHIP CRISIS

STEPHEN BLAHA

BLAHA RESEARCH

To My Wife Margaret

Some Other Books by Stephen Blaha

The Rises and Falls of Man – Destiny – 3000 AD: New Support for a Superorganism MACRO-THEORY of CIVILIZATIONS From CURRENT WORLD TRENDS and NEW Peruvian, Pre-Mayan, Mayan, Anatolian, and Early Egyptian Data, with a Projection to 3000 AD (Blaha Research, Auburn, NH, 2014).

SuperCivilizations: Civilizations as Superorganisms (McMann-Fisher Publishing, Auburn, NH, 2010).

The Rhythms of History: A Universal Theory of Civilizations (Pingree-Hill Publishing. Auburn, NH, 2002).

A Unified Quantitative Theory Of Civilizations and Societies: 9600 BC - 2100 AD (Pingree-Hill Publishing. Auburn, NH, 2004).

The Life Cycle of Civilizations (Pingree-Hill Publishing. Auburn, NH, 2002).

All the Multiverse! Starships Exploring the Endless Universes of the Cosmos using the Baryonic Force (Blaha Research, Auburn, NH, 2014)

All the Universe! Faster Than Light Tachyon Quark Starships & Particle Accelerators with the LHC as a Prototype Starship Drive Scientific Edition (Pingree-Hill Publishing, Auburn, NH, 2011).

Available on bn.com, Amazon.com, Amazon.co.uk and other international web sites as well as at better bookstores (through Ingram Distributors).

PREFACE

President Obama said in the past year that the United States does not necessarily have to be the leading country in the world. This book discusses the United States position as the World's leading country: the benefits, problems, and drawbacks.

It considers the impact of internal problems: unemployment, drugs, crime, violence and so on, on the leadership position of the United States.

The very strong impact of serious epidemics on the US is also described.

US foreign policy indecisiveness and weakness, and their impact on relations with allies and foes are detailed. We also consider specific foreign situations such as problems with Russia and China, the Ukraine, the China Seas confrontations, the possibility of a Russia-China pact to mutually support their aggressions, the Mexican and South American hidden drug wars, ISIS, the serious dilemma of dealing with Islam with the suggestion of American non-involvement as the best policy, the problem of North Korea, and the Iranian confrontation.

The serious impact of current events on American freedoms, and the mounting level of eavesdropping and internal spying on Americans, is considered. We also discuss the possibility of a drift towards tyranny and Presidential dictatorship.

We conclude by providing a brief evaluation of President Obama's successes and failures.

The United States was in a stage of rapid expansion until World War I with an overall positive view of the future and America's role in it as an increasingly powerful world leader with a moral stance as the leader of a world movement towards peace, prosperity and democracy. Subsequent to the war the United States entered a period of triumph and turmoil (a Time of Troubles in the jargon of Arnold Toynbee) – labor problems, recurrent economic problems, social unrest, conflict between the poor and the well off, and recently a sharp decline in the general view of the people that their children would have a better life.

The result is a form of breakdown in the American spirit that is reflected in all aspects of life in America. We examine the role of America as a world leader, both now and in the future, the proper course of action (strategy) that America should follow, and the internal issues that beset America and impact on its leadership role in the world. We shall also compare it to the British and Roman experiences as world leaders.

Herodotus, the "father" of History, said several times in his writings that some things "may not be spoken of." This stricture is implicit in several topics discussed in this book.

CONTENTS

1. WORLD LEADER OR PARTNER?　　1

1.1 The Benefits of Leadership... 3

1.2 The Negatives of Strong Leadership 4

1.3 Lessons from Past "World" Leading Nations........................... 5

    1.3.1 Ancient Rome when it was the Great Leader 6

    1.3.2 Great Britain when it was the World Leader 8

    1.3.3 How Does the United States Measure Up as a Leader Compared to Rome and Great Britain? 10

1.4 TV News Media Impact on the People and Presidency 13

1.5 Should the United States Continue as World Leader or Regress to a Leading Partner Role?..16

2. INTERNAL STABILITY OF THE UNITED STATES　　17

2.1 New Divisions Appearing in the United States........................17

2.2 Problems Leading to Divisions and National Instability 18

    2.2.1 Unemployment 18

    2.2.2 Drugs...19

    2.2.3 Dissatisfaction with Government..19

    2.2.4 Immigration and Illegal Entry...21

    2.2.5 Medical Insurance and Hospitals 22

    2.2.6 Breakdown of Law and Order 24

    2.2.7 Social Fragmentation – Class War..26

    2.2.8 Overpopulation 26

    2.2.9 Environmental degradation 27

    2,2,10 Homeless Children and Teens..28

2.3 The Breakdown of the Fabric of Society 30

3. WORLD-WIDE (EBOLA-LIKE) PLAGUES AND WARS   31

3.1 Possibility of Plague and War – History 31
3.2 Possible Plague and War in the Near Future.....................32
3.3 Vulnerability of the United States to a Bioweapons Plague followed by a Major War 33

4. IMPACT ON FOREIGN POLICY   34

4.1 Domestic Turmoil Limits Freedom of Action in Foreign Policy 35
4.2 Indecisive American Behavior makes Allies Uneasy and Enemies Adventurist 36
4.3 Weak Response to Aggression Leads to Growth in Enemy Power...37

5. SPECIFIC FOREIGN SITUATIONS   39

5.1 Ebola and Other Epidemics – An International Threat 39
5.2 Muslim Nation Building 40
    5.2.1 The War with ISIS.......................................41
    5.2.2 Let Islam Resolve its own Internal Conflicts! 43
    5.2.3 The Failed Strategy of Eliminating Muslim Dictators 45
5.3 A Possible Widening of the Ukraine Civil Struggle to a World War 46
    5.3.1 The Ukraine – The Beginning of Bigger Things?.............47
    5.3.2 Russia in Central Asia – Oil and Minerals 48
    5.3.3 The Arctic 48
    5.3.4 Eastern European Hegemony 49
5.4 A Chinese Expansionism.......................................49
    5.4.1 Central Asian Expansion................................50

5.4.2 South China Sea 51

5.4.3 Indian border/Kashmir...51

5.4.4 Eventually Siberia...52

5.5 A Russia-China Non-Aggression Pact Reminiscent of the Pre-World War II German-Russian Pact? 52

5.6 Mexican Non-Cooperation – Immigration and Drugs..............53

5.6.1 Drug Trade 53

5.6.2 Massive Immigration 54

5.6.3 Proposal for an American Response 54

5.7 Central America & Columbia/South America 56

5.8 The Iranian Conflict...57

5.9 The North Korean Confrontation...57

6. A TREND TOWARD A TOTALITARIAN UNITED STATES?   59

6.1 Recent Presidential Excesses....................................60

6.2 Totalitarianism and Unpopular Presidents 62

6.3 Totalitarianism and Popular Presidents..........................63

6.4 Protection from illegal Searches and Surveillance 65

6.5 The Trend towards a Totalitarian United States 67

6.6 President Obama – a Brief Evaluation 68

REFERENCES

INDEX

ABOUT THE AUTHOR

1. World Leader or Partner?

Greatness has a great price as the parade of great nations through history shows. The United States achieved a preeminent position in the world in the 1990's after the collapse of the Soviet Union.[1] There were minor annoyances: North Korea and Iran being the most prominent. But the world at large enjoyed a measure of peace although there were significant problems: environmental degradation, poverty, localized random violence, terrorism and so on.

Now the United States is facing a set of challenges that have led to a reduced standing in the world. Psychologically the greatest challenge would appear to be terrorism. Yet the activities of terrorists have been relatively minor compared to other challenges. Yes, the 911 World Trade Center disaster was significant and much to be regretted. But the sum of terrorist activities throughout the world in the past fourteen years is small compared to the tragic world wars, genocides, and lesser wars such as Korea and Vietnam not to mention many smaller scale conflicts which led to a significant loss of life.

The great disaster, in this writer's opinion, was the massive response to terrorism that has cost America many lives, large financial expenditures, and a serious decline in the freedom and privacy that we had previously enjoyed. The

---

[1] Despite the decline of Western Civilization as we discussed in the Preface. As the leading nation in Western Civilization the United States is part of this decline – a decline that is mirrored by the decline in the United Kingdom and Europe.

terrorists have succeeded in making America a "fearful" nation; "What will they do next?" is the constant thought of the people, the government and particularly the media who have an unholy obsession of dwelling on tragic terrorists events to the point of nausea.[2]

The growth of fear in America and the concomitant growth of fear of ground combat, are part of a psychologically weakening nation that has allowed other nations – Russia in the Ukraine, rebels in Iraq and Afghanistan, Iran, China in the East and South China Seas, Iran, and North Korea – to engage in adventures that have shown America to be unwilling to aid its friends and ready to give way to its enemies. The "No boots on the ground" policy is an invitation to opponents to do what they will, knowing that a supine America will not strongly oppose them.

Given the circumstances outlined above it is important to decide what America's role in the 21st century should be, and to consider the benefits and negatives of leadership, or of merely accepting the role of the "leading" partner of a coalition.

---

[2] The old America of the Wild West, the Civil War, and Teddy Roosevelt knew violence and reacted to it firmly, decisively and without useless lamenting in the press. The old America would have solved the terrorist security issue of air travel, not with very expensive airport security measures that are both bothersome and really not fool proof, but with passenger and crew action to put down any terrorist or passenger misbehavior. This approach has been successfully used in a number of incidents. Since passengers will always outnumber terrorists in a jet, we might consider arming respectable looking, responsible passengers on each jet with tasers and forego intensive security checks that can be evaded by clever terrorists. Stage coaches had men riding with shot guns and armed passengers and no security lines– a suggestive approach for air travel.

1.1 The Benefits of Leadership

Although some government leaders have voiced acceptance of a secondary role for America in the world, the majority of Americans wish America to reassert its world leadership. We have seen America take a back seat after World War I, partly due to President Wilson's illness, and then watched the old quarrels and conflicts of Europe set the stage for World War II. America cannot afford to abandon its leadership role because most nations in Asia and Africa as well as some in Europe have outstanding disagreements which would otherwise be resolved by might of arms in many cases. The consequence of this course of action is clear: the powerful will become stronger (Russia and China particularly), and rise to challenge a weaker America in the future.

The political/military benefits of an America maintaining its strength to lead the world and confront any challenge to world peace are clear. America must have a "prevent defense" to guarantee that no nation or combination of nations could threaten it in the future.

A secondary benefit that is not often stated is the enormous financial benefit that accrues to America as world leader: control of the world financial markets that enables it to survive its enormous debt burden, access to raw materials in Africa and Asia that a powerful hostile nation[3] might deny it, and the ability to support the financial needs of important allies particularly in Eastern Europe.

---

[3] China is presently making major efforts to obtain mineral rights in Africa. Some of these minerals are crucially needed for American industry and defense.

1.2 The Negatives of Strong Leadership

The role of being the leading nation in the world places major burdens on it. First it requires a strong military and the willingness to use it for just cause. Soldiers will die or become severely injured. We wish it would be otherwise. But we must realize as our forefathers did that one must pay for freedom in this world. Liberty, like everything, has a price. And the price can be the lives of fine young men and women.

If we choose to accept an air war-based policy of not using soldiers on the ground then adversaries can take advantage of this strategy by dispersing their armies and planes. Then air warfare becomes counterproductive – much expense, little benefit. A case in point that happened yesterday (September 23, 2014): American aircraft costing perhaps as much as one hundred million dollars bombed an ISIS installation destroying one light truck and caused other minor damage. If a jet were lost (costing perhaps thirty million dollars) and its pilot killed how can one justify that action?

An air war is only viable against troop and equipment concentrations. Thereby one can prevent significant military moves by an enemy and keep the enemy unbalanced. Naturally an enemy would know this, and disperse its troops and equipment probably within non-combatant populations. Then low cost American drones would provide a suitable attack vehicle.

The use of American ground forces only makes sense if the land they capture remains in American or American ally hands. We have seen in Iraq that the land for which so many lives were lost, and so much money spent, is now in the hands of various factions most of whom are hostile to the United States. The entry of the United States into a war with a petty dictator, such as the Iraq war was, is bad strategy. Rather an air war with no intent of capturing land is a better strategy. The Iraq of Saddam Hussein with its large army and air force was ideally suited for this purpose as the first war with Iraq showed.

Unlike World War II's aftermath when Germany and Italy were occupied and reformed, warfare today with Islamic countries and populations[4] will only yield short term benefits. Thus air wars, to prevent growth in military strength, are the only reasonable choice for America.

We see that the negative factors in maintaining American world leadership are the cost of a large military establishment, the lives that will be lost in war, the cost of propping up financially weak allies, and the cost of a world-wide policing role.

Another negative is the need to have distasteful dictatorships as allies and to tolerate their forms of government.

Above all a wise and humane overall strategy is required that will tolerate minimal violence against America (at least for a time) and not be carried away by emotion. We cannot afford "Remember the Maine" style media excesses to cause strategic errors to placate an aroused American populace. The President and Congress should be above that sort of pressure.

1.3 Lessons from Past "World" Leading Nations

When considering the present and future situation of America we should be mindful of lessons of past great leading nations.[5] The past great "world" leading nations are many. They dominated various regions of the world for periods of time. The

---

[4] And other countries whose culture and religion are anti-American, and will remain so indefinitely.

[5] The discussions of this section are abbreviated and designed to serve the purpose of the chapter. There are many excellent books covering the topics discussed here briefly that provide greater detail.

ones with which we are most familiar are ancient Rome, and Great Britain. We will overview their development with a view towards better understanding their rise to leadership and subsequent decline. While we hope the United States will forever be the world's inspiration and leader, history indicates that leading nations eventually decline for one reason or another. One cannot blind oneself to the mortality of people and of nations.

1.3.1 Ancient Rome when it was the Great Leader

Rome began as a small nation – deeply religious although not Christian – and with a strict code of conduct that forbade works of art such as statutes[6] and music as promoting effeminacy. Partly because of its superior military techniques (not equipment but methods of warfare), and partly because some nations wished to join Rome because of its quasi-democratic government and their desire for Rome's protection, Rome grew to greatness as the leader/ruler of the Mediterranean world.

Then its wealth attracted immigrants (barbarians) and long lasting enemies (the Parthian Empire). Most importantly a decline in its best manpower occurred due to the creation of vast estates using slaves rather than the sturdy Roman farmers that were the stout heart of the formerly formidable Roman Legions. Its wealth was also depleted by the silk trade and the cost of defending a vast territory with mercenaries.

A side effect of Rome's use of mercenaries, and its continuous wars to defend its borders, was the transfer of its

---

[6] Rome did collect the statutes of the gods of cities and nations they conquered for placement in their temples.

military techniques to its adversaries and future adversaries (barbarians) who eventually bought Rome to its knees.

What can we learn from the Roman experience?

1) Excessive wealth saps the strength of a people. Its working class is the soul of its military strength and must not be degraded for financial or other reasons;

2) Fighting enemies over long periods of time results in a technology transfer to enemies thus reducing the advantage of the leader nation;

3) The entrance of "barbarians" and their use in war rather than the leader's people eventually leads to a decline in the military strength of the leader;

4) The leader's financial strength is a critical part of the continuation of leadership.

Point 4 is very well illustrated by the fall of the Eastern (Byzantine) Roman Empire. The Empire's very rich citizens refused to loan money to the government to pay for its defense against the Turks and the Empire fell.

Rome had a series of choices to make about its expansion to leadership of the Mediterranean world. It developed temporary alliances that usually ended in absorption into the Roman Empire. Its temporary partners tended to become antagonistic to Rome resulting in eventual Roman conquest.

Carthage was a major opponent of Rome. Its first two wars with Rome challenged Rome strongly. Hannibal raged through Italy and threatened the city of Rome seriously. After its second defeat Carthage abandoned military confrontations with Rome and concentrated on commerce with great success. Its success aroused the envy of Rome ("Carthago delenda est" was frequently heard in the Roman Senate). Rome then proceeded to make war on Carthage and after victory sowed the soil of Carthage with salt so it would never rise again.

In a sense Rome's military superiority, and the weakness of most other Mediterranean nations, made a rise to a dominant leadership position more or less inevitable. Its primary long lasting rival was the Parthian Empire. Later in its history German tribes, the Huns and other bordering powers rose to challenge it and eventually conquered it.

The enormous wealth it acquired, particularly through its conquest of Egypt, created the greatness of Rome, and, as Gibbons remarks, led to the happiest age of Man up to the 19th century. On that basis one can only conclude that Rome as the leader was much better than the alternative of a conglomeration of quarrelsome Mediterranean nations.

1.3.2 Great Britain when it was the World Leader

Great Britain, like Rome, seems to have developed a populace with a strong character. The Romans when they conquered England remarked at the strictness with which British children were raised – rather extraordinary considering the toughness of the Romans.

The strength of character of the British is illustrated by a line from a mid-20th century British movie[7] about the British conquest of the Sudan in the late 19th century. In an opening scene, at a dinner of old British comrades from the Battle of Balaklava (the scene of the famous Charge of the Light Brigade) in the Crimea, the most prominent guest, General Burroughs,

---

[7] "Four Feathers" a movie directed by Zoltan Korda, a Hungarian émigré to Great Britain.

the leader of the charge, remarked of a fellow officer, "Lost his arm in the battle. Ruined his cricket." This understated view of a tragic injury reflects the hardy spirit of the British people as does their heroic response to the Blitz in World War II.

This internal fortitude led over time to the British challenge to the dominance of Spain first by its daring pirates attacks on Spanish treasure ships coming from America, then by the defeat of the Spanish Armada, and subsequently by the creation of a great navy that led Britain to develop a far-flung empire throughout the world. The British army, particularly in the 19th century, also was very successful in colonial wars through tough discipline, the use of the "British square" defensive tactics, and the use of machine guns later in the 19th century to overwhelm third world armies.

Britain started the 19th century as a partner with Prussia, Russia, and the Austro-Hungarian Empire to defeat Napoleonic France. It then developed its Empire primarily in Asia and Africa but also Canada and Australia while European powers were wrangling for power in Europe.

A major component of Britain's success was to promote divisions between its enemies to weaken them and make them easier to conquer, and also the use of native troops and minor potentates to augment its military operations. At the end of the 19th century Great Britain ruled a world-wide empire, had acquired enormous wealth, and was effectively the leader of the world.

Great Britain benefited enormously from its rise to de facto world leader. However, the subsequent world wars and the emergence of the United States due to its large size, population and resources led to United States world leadership although it was challenged by a competing Soviet Union.

1.3.3 How Does the United States Measure Up as a Leader Compared to Rome and Great Britain?

The United States has been the leader of the Free World since World War II, and World Leader in the 1990's. If one compares the United States to Rome and Great Britain as a world leader then there are many points of similarity.

They all started with a population with a strong moral character and underwent a difficult development through wars and invasions by enemies. In the case of the United States there were continuous wars with American Indian tribes that parallel the Roman experience in a sense – except for their advantage in firearms and in farming techniques.[8] The hardy, gritty people that developed from this experience grew to be strong and capable, as became evident in the Civil War and the westward expansion to the Pacific.

The entry into World War I showed the formidable capabilities of the United States. Its role in World War II confirmed its status as the strongest nation in the world despite Communist efforts to undermine it.

The collapse of the Soviet Union in 1990 left the United States without a rival for world leadership. There was an expectation that the world was entering an age of peace and stability.

This expectation ended in 2001 when terrorists destroyed the New York World Trade buildings. It then became clear to Americans that there was great hatred for the United States and other countries of Western Civilization in the Muslim world. The countries of the West were blamed for the poverty

---

[8] American Indians were in an intermediate stage between hunter-gatherer and farming. There are some diaries of puritan settlers comparing the relative plenty of the puritans due to their farming with the sparse, unsettled life of the Indian tribes.

and social ills of the Muslim world. And there was a residue of the religious hatred for Christians and Jews that has permeated the Muslim world for almost fifteen hundred years. The United States embarked on a campaign to combat Muslim terrorists that has lasted for fourteen years with some victories: temporary conquests of Iraq and Afghanistan and the destruction of some terrorists and terrorist camps. However the United States is now realizing that the conflict with Muslim terrorism is long term and will probably last for generations.

The people of Islam have spoken for many generations of the "Islamic Nation" – a great country composed of all currently separate Muslim nations. If this dream were realized then Western Civilization would then face a major foe as it did in the Middle Ages when Islam almost conquered Europe. The medieval threat began to end when the Venetian fleet defeated a major Muslim fleet at the Battle of Lepanto. The conflict continued for several hundred years with the Western nations eventually winning with superior weapons and tactics.

Now the West faces the beginning of another Muslim challenge at the terrorist level. If a unified Muslim force develops, as ISIS currently threatens to become, then a new phase of conflict will begin. This prospect has aroused Western nations to begin an air war to suppress ISIS. It will probably succeed. But it is almost certain that new Muslim organizations will arise to fight the West. As long as the West has a strong military it will win. Eventually, perhaps in about five hundred years, an Islamic Nation will arise that might extend from Indonesia to Africa. Then Western Civilization would be in danger of total defeat.

The Roman and British experiences, and the long history of Islamic-Western conflict, lead to the following points regarding successful leadership:

1. Since excessive wealth and leisure saps the strength of a people the West must continue to engage in major manufacturing, mining and farming enterprises. We cannot become mere consumers of cheaply made foreign products based on cheap labor. Thus Western Civilization will continue to have a strong yeomanry for war if it should become necessary.

2. Fighting enemies over long periods of time would result in a technology transfer to enemies and reduce the competitive advantage of the leader nation – the United States – and other Western nations. In the case of Islam, Western nations should only defend their important interests and not enter into internal disputes between and within Islamic countries. At the present time this policy would suggest an exit from interference of any kind in Syria and Iraq except for humanitarian gifts of medical supplies. Let the Muslims fight their own battles. This policy would enable the West to avoid Islamic charges of "Crusaderism." Will Western non-involvement lead to the emergence of a formidable adversary? We view this as highly unlikely in view of the past history of Islam and the Shia-Sunni divide. In the cases of Russia and China a different course should be pursued since these nations are interested in mundane self-interest, and do not have a strong religious purpose as Islam does, Any aggression on their part should be met strongly with a speedy response that will reassure allies and give these

adversaries pause for thought before engaging in aggression.

3. The entrance of immigrants from non-Western nations must be strictly limited as they will have an increasingly divisive effect on Western politics. These considerations apply to Mexican, Central American and South American immigrants as well. At present these immigrants strain the finances of the countries which they enter by their need for social/medical services; contribute to unemployment and low pay for native workers – particularly young entrants into the labor markets; and over the long term they will alter Western culture in unhappy ways judging by the cultures of the lands from which they come.

4. The leading nations' financial strength must grow from its present low point to enable these nations support of government services such as medical care and care for the elderly. In addition financial strength is a prerequisite for a strong military for defense. The best method to increase financial strength is a tariff wall[9] to mitigate the trade advantages of low cost labor nations. Reasonably set tariffs will enable domestic industry to compete successfully with low labor cost foreign industry, and thus to grow and prosper. A strong industrial base is a requirement for a strong nation.

1.4 TV News Media Impact on the People and Presidency

Today several TV stations present news on a 24/7 basis tirelessly dredging up "new" news and repeatedly presenting it

---

[9] See Blaha (2013b) for a detailed proposal.

in a barrage on the American public. Crime stories are mined for every sordid detail. International news is exhaustively and repeatedly re-presented throughout the day. The net result is the saturation of the American public to such an extent that it should almost be viewed as a form of "brainwashing." While news people have a right to speak under the Constitution it is clear that the over coverage of events, to which they are forced, in order to fill their twenty-four hour days has some serious deleterious effects. The most prominent of these bad effects is the "encouragement" of copycat crimes both within the country and abroad. We only need note the brutal beheadings that ISIS perpetrated KNOWING they would get extensive world-wide news coverage. Other international copycat misdeeds have occurred in the past. And one only need note the "benefits" that Iran and North Korea derive from outrageous statements. Without repetitious international news coverage these countries would be much less likely to present their threats and tirades. Modest coverage, or ignoring their blather, would end their dominance of the news.

A more pernicious effect of 24/7 international (and national) over coverage is the effect on American political leaders. The news media overly influence the American public on numerous occasions which, in turn, causes our political leaders, and the President, to take stances designed to please the public. These stances are often not in the best interest of the American people. For example, the known public dislike of sending troops abroad led President Obama to announce a "No boots on the ground" policy.[10] While one does necessarily

---

[10] President Obama should have resisted the pressure to make this announcement. It gave comfort to our enemies and despair to our friends. A stronger president such as Harry Truman would have kept silence in the interests of national security. Obama's

disagree with that policy, the announcement of it gives courage to our opponents, stimulates them to further misdeeds, limits the freedom of action of our leaders, and consequently could actually lead to American boots on the ground. A wise policy is NOT to announce policy in advance. A policy of discrete silence is almost impossible due to the media barrage for information from the President and other leaders. The World War II slogan, "Loose lips sinks ships" is well to bear in mind.

The pressure brought to bear on the President by the new media borders on bullying to the detriment of the security of the United States.

Those who may think that this section is overstated should remember the cause of the Spanish-American War in 1898. The American warship Maine sank in Havana harbor under mysterious circumstances that were not proven to be an attack by Spain. The news media (the "Yellow Journalists" leaped on this event, paraded the slogan "Remember the Maine" repeatedly in their headlines and news stories. The result was a war of doubtful long term benefit to the United States followed by insurrections in conquered Spanish territories: the Philippines and Puerto Rico (that lasted into the 1950's in the case of Puerto Rico.) Joseph Pulitzer and William Hearst were the leading muck raking journalists who instigated this war. If newspapers had such strength then, how much more influential are TV news media today?

One can hope that 24/7 news media realize their impact and that over coverage of events should be carefully self-

---

pronouncement is understandable because it reflected the feelings of the majority of the American people. However a great leader leads with courage and does not appease the public. He should have remained silent on this issue and braved the brunt of public criticism.

monitored and self-policed by the media. Frankly, hour-length evening news programs as we had until recently (such as those of Walter Cronkite, and Huntley-Brinkley) should be brought back so that the American public will not be drowned in irrelevant repetition and "brain washing" to fill TV time for the benefit of commercials. American political leaders should go about their business without uninformed public pressure induced by the necessarily partial knowledge of the media.

1.5 Should the United States Continue as World Leader or Regress to a Leading Partner Role?

Yes. The alternative choices, Russia and China, have repressive governments and an aggressive expansionary foreign policy. A coalition or partnership approach does not work well because of conflicts in the goals and approaches of the partners. Realistically any successful partnership is only as effective as its leading member. Thus in today's world a partnership is disguised leadership which influences the other members of the partnership in the interests of solidarity.

The reader should remember a paraphrase of Gibbon's comment on Rome:

> *America's leadership has resulted in the happiest time in history for the largest number of Mankind.*

Internal stability is a prerequisite for the continued role of the United States as world leader. We consider the problems and stability of the United States in the next chapter.

2. Internal Stability of the United States

The ability of the United States to maintain its role as world leader depends on the strength and unity of the American people. Recently it has become clear that internal divisions within the American people have been increasing. In the 20th century the primary long lasting division was racial. The secondary division was between the wealthy and the lower middle class workers.

2.1 New Divisions Appearing in the United States

Today it is apparent that there are new divisions within Americans. Some of these new, or sharper, divisions are: immigrants vs. native born Americans, the development of large gangs that wish to "partner" with government,[11] the separation of Americans wishing more government benefits vs. Americans seeking to lower benefits or at least maintain the status quo, and the division between Americans wanting lower taxes and less government (such as the Tea Party) vs. those who wish to maintain the current government programs and tax structure (with perhaps minimal changes). In this chapter we will examine some of the problems these divisions reflect and the social causes that motivate them.

---

[11] Meaning they wish to obey laws of their choice, have their own laws, and have a direct role in government.

2.2 Problems Leading to Divisions and National Instability

There are many problems leading to difficulties for the United States to maintain its position as world leader. In this section we will briefly discuss them. More detail on specific problems with proposed solutions can be found in Blaha (2013b) and (2014c). The below list is incomplete and not ranked by order of severity.

2.2.1 Unemployment

The United States made an agreement with China in 1994 giving it most favored nation status in trading. This agreement opened the door further to a flood of Chinese goods made with low cost and slave labor. The net result was a severe decline in American manufacturing that has led to high unemployment rates for unskilled American labor and for young people wanting entry level positions. This problem was further exacerbated by the use of Indian programmers and help line workers. While it is good that these low income countries received employment opportunities, it has had a disastrous effect on the job prospects of American young people and unskilled labor.

A further problem that has weakened the social stability of the United States is the decline in big industries such as automobiles and computer manufacturers that has eliminated the possibility of stable, lifetime jobs for American workers. The resulting uncertainty and unemployment has unhinged part of the social stability that has been a cornerstone of the American worker community.

Welfare payments, unemployment benefits and mandatory cash buyouts to eliminate workers have not mitigated the social uncertainty of a declining, unstable job market.

2.2.2 Drugs

The widespread and still increasing use of illegal drugs particularly by young people will have major direct and indirect consequences for America's stability and capabilities as the world leader. The direct effects include: the degradation of the skills, abilities and education of young people; the bad impact of drugs on the military skills of the armed forces; a large, expensive prison population; and a massive financial burden for law enforcement, crime, and drug traffic interdiction at the trillion dollar level. The indirect effects include: the degradation of the moral/ethical level of the population; lower worker quality resulting in manufacturing problems; increased law enforcement problems; an increase in psychological problems in the population; and a major decline in child rearing due to large numbers of druggie parents.

The cumulative result is a weaker country whose leadership capabilities are declining significantly.

2.2.3 Dissatisfaction with Government

The decline in the political leadership of the Unite States is obvious and a source of gallows humor in political campaigns and on TV programs. The corruption of the Congress due to influence peddling by domestic companies *and foreign countries* is known to all. "Every congressman retires rich" is a sad commentary on the Congress. The result is defective laws and pork barrel funding that expropriates money from the taxpayers and that leads to expensive, misguided funding of our military with an obvious weakening effect on the people and our defense capabilities.

The Executive branch of the federal government is similarly beset with problems similar to those of the Congress. The tardy actions of the Executive branch, and their missteps, seriously undermine the leadership role of the country.

The Supreme Court which has been the victim of political maneuvering by the Congress and Presidents in recent years, is not at the level of quality of previous Supreme Courts. Where are the Oliver Wendell Holmes', the Brandeis', and so on that led the Supreme Court with justice and common sense? Today's Supreme Court does not recognize or respond to the continuing crisis of law enforcement in this country. The result is an insecure populace. The insecurity is obvious from the massive sale of guns and the obsession with home defense of most Americans.

The federal government in all its branches is contributing to the decline of America in the world.

Local governments are somewhat better in their honesty and commitment to better government and education. However there is a growing corruption problem in local government due to real estate and business influence peddling. The drug problem, with its vast flow of illegal money, is also affecting local government – particularly police departments.

It is said, "A people gets the government it deserves." Given this statement we see the American people are at fault and, in these difficult times, are becoming more greedy, less conscientious, and less honest.

2.2.4 Immigration and Illegal Entry

The United States is being inundated with legal and illegal immigrants. The immigrants are coming here to work and improve the living standards of themselves and their children. One cannot fault these people for their desire for a better life. America has always had that role as the "encouragement of the world" in the words of Abraham Lincoln.

However the present condition of the United States, and its future condition, raises the question whether large scale immigration is good for the future of the country. The United States is filled. We are no longer a country in need of more people to grow.

The new immigrants entering the United States bring with them an expanded demand for expensive health services at a time when health costs are placing an ever increasing burden on the people and the economy. They also significantly increase law enforcement and other governmental expenses.

But the greatest problem is that they take jobs from Americans by accepting lower wages and working conditions. As a result they increase unemployment – particularly for young entry level Americans who already have a depression era unemployment rate of about 25%.

Many of the new immigrants decline to assimilate into the American way of life and government unlike earlier generations. Muslim and Hispanic immigrants tend to demand acceptance of their dress and customs and the use of their languages in public schools. The growth of the Hispanic population in the American Southwest and California could be viewed as a peaceful reconquest of these regions by Mexico.

Thus the immigrant invasion by its sheer size is creating a new divisive force in the United States. This divisiveness is very evident in the political maneuvering by political parties over immigration. The basis of this maneuvering is voting power. Historically it has been a grave error to allow foreign people to influence the politics of a nation. A good example of this fact is Rome where immigrants (barbarians) came to work and be soldiers, but who went on to conquer Rome. For example, Attila the Hun came to Rome to live and learn, returned to Hungary, and came back to Rome as a conqueror.

2.2.5 Medical Insurance and Hospitals

The greatest concern of both senior citizens and working age people (excepting employment worries) is health insurance. It is extremely expensive and inflating rapidly. Government has recognized this concern with Medicare, Medicaid, ObamaCare, and other programs. These programs aid the people but represent an enormous, and increasing, cost to federal and state governments that can only be met by increasing taxes.

Unfortunately the methods of these programs are subject to serious criticism. Many parts of these programs are difficult to understand by the average citizen. Many stipulations in these programs make it difficult if not impossible for a patient to know the extent and amount of coverage. For example, a major drug chain is not able to tell a customer the cost of an insurance covered drug until the sale is rung up on the cash register. There are many worse cases of lack of knowledge of insurance program coverage. Coverage is also often quixotic – some medical expenses are covered – some are not. Again pharmacy drugs are a good example: some prescribed drugs are covered, some prescribed drugs of equal importance are not.

As a result medical insurance programs are not liked by the majority of the American people and are a major cause of dissatisfaction with government. This dissatisfaction is enhanced by the very excellent medical insurance afforded to the President and Congress.

In addition to the medical insurance issue there are major problems with doctor and hospital staff practices. Anyone who has been hospitalized, or had family members hospitalized, has probably seen the indifference, and/or lack of care and callous treatment of many nursing staff. Partly this is due to insufficient staff but more often it is due to lack of concern after treating many patients. (In fairness we note some nursing staff members are concerned and do their job properly.) Complaints about staff to management often lead to subtle retaliation by nursing staff. Truly, a patient is at the mercy of nursing staff who often base their caregiving on their feelings about the patient.

Doctors also would appear to fairly often show indifference to patient's needs and suffering. Doctors also frequently engage in what appears to be bad procedures. For example, some doctors group a full day of operations on patients so that they can have days off. Do the fifth through the tenth patients being operated on towards the end of a day really have a well-rested, alert doctor performing the procedure? Could this practice be connected to the relatively numerous mistakes in operations? Has any medical research group studied the effects of this fairly common practice?

American medicine may be among the best in the world but there are significant problems in medical insurance, hospitals, and in doctor's practices that raise doubts in the minds of the citizenry.

2.2.6 Breakdown of Law and Order

The decline in employment, particularly of young people (25% unemployed), has led to an increase of crime and violence in the United States. Due to a misguided sense of pity, the police, and the courts, have taken a more lenient attitude to petty crime in particular, not realizing that petty crime often leads perpetrators to major crime. There is also a feeling that only major crime is worthy to take to court. Court cases are expensive for towns and cities.

The net result is that there is a significant growth in petty crime and in "subtle" crime where the crime is not clearly evident.[12] The existence of this sort of crime is not new but the increasing prevalence of these crimes (stimulated partly by the drug epidemic) is cause for alarm. They lead to a pervasive uneasiness that is partly the reason for the huge increase in gun sales.

Another growing form of crime is violence in the schools. Bullying and violence in schools are not new. But the trend is alarming – particularly the number of shooting instances and student deaths. To some extent one has to question the extensive media coverage of these events and their possible effect – copycat crimes. Again we see the insecurity in parents, students and teachers that contributes to the general unease of the country.

A related aspect of youth violence is the regrowth of gangs. Gangs are often involved in drug dealing, extortion and violence. They frequently implement a code of silence in the areas where they operate with threats against nearby residents

---

[12] An example of this sort of crime is a burglary where only some items of "little" value are stolen and the victim is unaware of the loss. This type of crime is often not reported to police.

and their relatives. The use of cell phones and cooperation with gangs in other areas creates a national threat. One can view this coordinated gang movement as a form of internal terrorism. One gang member in Minnesota was quoted on national TV as expressing the wish that his gang could be affiliated with government. The gang movement is evolving into a loosely integrated "black market government" and our government appears unable to deal with this problem just as they have difficulties with international terrorism.

One might hope that local police forces could cope with violence and the gangs but the police are handicapped by excessive adverse publicity, police corruption, excessively restrictive laws, gang intimidation of police, and sometimes excessive use of force and/or racism that is played up in the media to such an extent that legitimate police efforts are forestalled for fear of bad publicity.

Another related issue is a misguided and sometimes corrupt legal system – particularly in the lower courts. While most judges are conscientiously deciding cases there is an increasing tendency for judges to make decisions out of fear of retaliation by gangs and organized crime. District attorneys and prosecutors face a similar problem of intimidation and retaliation. A few years ago a Washington state District Attorney was assassinated in his own home by criminal elements as yet unidentified. Yet again the citizenry has cause for alarm at the drift of the country towards lawlessness.

The combined effect of the above mentioned problems is to lower the people's regard for the government and to further increase the downward trend of American morality.

2.2.7 Social Fragmentation – Class War

It has become quite clear to the American people that the upward social mobility that resulted from the GI Bill of Rights after World War II and continued into the 1990's is not as extensive today as it was in the past. Most lower income people view themselves, and their children, as locked at their current level due to the tight financial situation of the country for the foreseeable future.

As a result it appears to most that America is no longer the land of opportunity that it once was. Instead a distinct class structure is emerging and is a subject of discussion as it wasn't before the economic downfall beginning in 2000.

A class structure will cause a deterioration in America's role as the world leader and reduce the social cohesion that has been evident in the wars of the 20th century. (The Vietnam War was admittedly divisive but not as a class issue but as moral and foreign policy issues.) The promotion of upward mobility and job growth would greatly benefit America's leadership role in the world and be "the encouragement of the world" as Lincoln so aptly put it in the last Lincoln-Douglas debate for an 1858 Illinois Senate seat.

2.2.8 Overpopulation

If one travels the country as this author has repeatedly done in the past fifteen years then it is clear that the habitable parts of the country are well populated and certain parts could be viewed as over-populated. If we consider the purposes of immigration we see that the socially beneficial role is to fill an "empty" country for the benefit of the country's growth and prosperity.

At present the United States has significant unemployment – particularly for young people – and does not need to enlarge the population – particularly when new immigrants will increase the burdens of government and social services.

Therefore, it seems reasonable to severely limit immigration to critical skilled workers and to strictly enforce immigration laws to prevent further illegal immigration. Every time a native born American citizen loses a job to an illegal it is a disservice to his family and contributes to a weakening of the American social fabric. In one hundred years at present growth rates America's population will approach one billion inhabitants. Then, an extrapolation of the present economy suggests we will be comparable to China and India with a large population in poverty. That is not the America that can lead the world.

2.2.9 Environmental degradation

For most of its history the United States has relied on two methods of waste disposal: dilution of waste materials such as letting toxic waste flow into rivers and thence the ocean and burying waste in dumps since the country was blessed with much open land. These methods are no longer viable. Waste dispersed in water has come back to us through the food chain: fish containing toxic metals such as mercury, ground water containing low concentrations of toxic chemicals that appear to be playing a role in the large increase in certain types of cancer and the large increase in birth defects[13] and autism.

Attempts are being made to reverse environmental degradation. But the attempts are doing little more than

---

[13] Russia is the classic example of this problem. Half the children being born in Russia have birth defects – the result of decades of unrestricted pollution.

stabilizing the environment from further deterioration. There are some showcase bright spots. But the century of large scale pollution will be very costly to undo and will require a major change in the habits of the people as well as industry.

Meanwhile the country must deal with a large number of uneducable youth for the foreseeable future. Many of these young people have turned to drugs and crime – and increasing anti-social behavior as we see in the almost daily barrage of school crimes, murders, and what is politely termed bullying.

Older people also are being agitated by pollution related diseases and the continuing cascade of bad news about schools and medical care necessitated by exposure to pollutants. The large number of commercials from law firms seeking clients victimized by pollution illustrates the magnitude of this problem.

The net result of environmental decline is a decline in the American spirit that can only adversely affect America's world leadership role.

2,2,10 Homeless Children and Teens

From the viewpoint of compassion this topic should be at the top of this section. A recent study concluded that one American child out of thirty is homeless. These children (and teens) live in misery: often cold, poorly clothed, hungry, in need of medical and dental care, often sexually molested and brutalized by adults and other homeless children, used as slave labor, victimized by drugs, forced to move frequently from the temporary shelters they find in basements, attics, and industrial buildings, and led into crime and depravity.

What is their future? Early death, crime, depravity, prostitution, prison, homelessness, poverty, and little or no chance of emerging into a decent life.

How do we help these children and teens at present? Most are hidden and their plight conveniently ignored by people and government. Ignorance spares us the guilt and we congratulate ourselves on how we are not living in the horrors of the 19th century with debtor's prisons, work houses and so on.

The efforts we do make: homes and shelters for the known homeless children and families salve our consciences and allow us to forget these places are often the scenes of brutality, sexual molestation, slow starvation, poor clothing and lack of heat. The people that run these facilities are often little better than criminals. They do it "for the money."

What follows in the lives of these children and teens? Their most likely future is poverty, degradation, drugs and crime. They become the soldiers of crime and violence helping to perpetuate the cycle of poverty and crime.

Is there a remedy? It does not appear likely under current American circumstances.[14] The wave of drugs and violence occurring in America, together with the financially strapped position of the American government, makes the creation, and staffing, of good shelters for homeless children and teens almost impossible. This point is substantiated by the poor care given in most shelters now by an often indifferent and uncaring staff.

Long term we see this 3% of American children growing to be a blight on the American people that can only be corrected

---

[14] It is ironic to see American celebrities asking for money on TV to help children in foreign countries who are often in better circumstances than homeless American children. The only frequent appeals for help for American children are those of ST. Jude's Children's Hospital for funds to help American children with cancer. Homeless American children are an inconvenient embarrassment, apparently, for celebrities to work for.

by more police and more prisons. The price for this failure to act will be enormously larger in the future.

2.3 The Breakdown of the Fabric of Society

The many causes of national dismay listed in section 2.2 shows that our America is undergoing a slowly rolling breakdown that only became apparent with the tragic terrorist attack of 9/11 and the severe economic decline that also became evident about that time. The affluent 1990's gave way to an America that only saved itself from a severe depression by a massive expenditure of the national wealth.

All Americans living in the period after the year 2000 feel the change in national temperament and the drop in national spirit and unity. Potential enemies and Islamic terrorist organizations have sensed decline and are seeking to take advantage of it. The most significant example of this new state of affairs is Russian adventurism: the invasions of Georgia and the Ukraine, Russian bomber flights near Alaska and the Gulf of Mexico, and Russian bomber flights near northern Europe. These sorties are an attempt to intimidate the American and European governments. Our weak response (economic restrictions) and the "no boots on the ground" announced policy can only encourage further aggression. Since the majority of the American people are supportive of this response level we can expect to see an increase in hostilities from foes.

It is easy to trod on a supine America. Perhaps we should reread Tom Paine's pamphlet, *Common Sense*, that inspired the first generation of Americans to fight against the then leading nation in the world.

3. World-Wide (Ebola-like) Plagues and Wars

3.1 Possibility of Plague and War – History

An often repeated phrase that is evidenced by past events is "History repeats itself." Today we are confronted with the possibility of a plague – the Ebola epidemic – that appears to be increasing in West Africa and reaching out to other parts of the world. Simultaneously we have serious small "wars" in progress in the Middle East, the Ukraine and possibly the East and South China Seas that have the potential to become major conflicts leading to the possibility of a combination of plague and war.

This combination of events has occurred in the past – usually with disastrous results. The first noteworthy European combination of plague and war with striking consequences was the outbreak of plague in Athens in 430 BC in the midst of a series of wars between Athens, a sea-based power and Sparta, a land-based power. Between 1/3 and 2/3 of the Athenians died causing a major deterioration in Athens' ability to wage war. The plague was so virulent that the Spartans who launched another episode of war against Athens withdrew from the conflict because their renowned soldiers were afraid to contract the plague from Athenians in battle with them. Many historians view this plague as a major factor in the defeat of Athens – a defeat that led Spartan allies such as Corinth to call for the razing of Athens and the enslavement and dispersal of the Athenian people, which the Spartans refused to do. Athens, much destroyed, was saved from total destruction.

Another combination of plague and war occurred in the latter days of the Roman Empire. The empire was much weakened but survived for another century or so.

The third combination of plague and war occurred during World War I. The plague was known as the Spanish Flu and perhaps a hundred million people died. The existence of the war and the movement of people and troops helped spread this epidemic.

There are undoubtedly other similar cases of plague and war in history in various parts of the world. The combination of these tragic events is not necessarily accidental in many cases. The exacerbated epidemic in Athens was caused by people crowding into Athens for the protection of its walls. An overcrowded Athens aided the spread of the plague. Similarly the spread of the Spanish Flu was enhanced by the movements of people caused by the war and the difficulty of fighting the flu under war-time conditions.

3.2 Possible Plague and War in the Near Future

We are now faced with a serious epidemic that is presently largely confined to West Africa. As I write the epidemic is still increasing in most of the infected West African countries. Interestingly it is thought Ebola in Man was started by one person eating infected "bush meat."

Naturally many who have the money to leave the infected areas, and are not showing signs of the infection as yet, are trying to leave the infected areas and go to other parts of Africa or Europe or the United States. Tendrils of the epidemic have appeared in the United States and other countries.

Epidemics can be easily spread far and wide by air travel.

3.3 Vulnerability of the United States to a Bioweapons Plague followed by a Major War

Ebola apparently has an approximately 50% mortality rate. If Ebola raged in the United States it is reasonable that at least 1/3 of the population would die. The result would be a seriously weakened military, the destruction of transportation and the economy, and the loss of a significant fraction of the work force. Recovery from these ills would be slow and the United States would be vulnerable to a massive influx of immigrants and to a possible invasion. The aforementioned Athenian example illustrates the potential havoc a plague would cause. Greece took more than a hundred years of poverty to recover from the Athenian plague.

Conquest by a foreign power, brutal as some potential enemies are, would cause major suffering in the American people and destroy the belief that America is a blessed nation under God.

The possibility exists that a foreign power might use a plague bioweapon to weaken the United States to enable an easy conquest with most of the United States still intact and most Americans dead. The inoculation of the enemy's troops with a protective vaccine would allow a rapid entry of enemy forces.

4. Impact on Foreign Policy

The impact of the conditions described in preceding chapters on the United States and its posture in the world is profound. America has traditionally been a peace loving country. George Washington's Farewell Address set the tone for this position with his comment to avoid foreign entanglements.

This posture has served America well up to the time of the Spanish-American War. The United States grew by westward expansion and had only a short war with Mexico. The Monroe Doctrine served notice on European powers to not engage in American adventures. It was largely obeyed except for Napoleon III's short-lived Mexican conquest.

Today the United States has, and seeks, allies throughout the world. Due to its world-wide interests, and the lessons learned from pre-World War isolationism, it has no choice but to have foreign entanglements.

However, it is apparent that the United States has only been successful in 20th century wars when it is first attacked by a foreign enemy. The Spanish-American War was started by the "Remember the Maine" newspaper campaign following the sinking of the battleship Maine in Cuba. The entry into World War I was due to unrestricted German submarine attacks on American ships. World War II followed the attack on Pearl Harbor. The Korean War was started by the North Korean attack on American soldiers stationed in South Korea. The Iraqi wars were the result of belligerence and terrorist threats from Iraq and terrorist organizations within it. The lone exception was the

Vietnamese War which had only communist containment as its motive and American withdrawal as the result.

The message of these historic wars is that the key to American strength in foreign affairs is a united America. Victory requires unity. This is sadly lacking today.

4.1 Domestic Turmoil Limits Freedom of Action in Foreign Policy

The President and Congress are well aware of the disappointment of Americans over the news from Iraq and Afghanistan. To see the conflicts, the anti-Americanism, and the failure of the American trained armies to control their countries shows the enormous waste of Americans lost in combat and the waste of trillions of dollars conquering and administering these countries.

This failure and the emergence of new terrorist groups such as ISIS have generated dismay and disarray in the American people. Together with the other major issues generating discord in the country the American government has been forced to take a public stance to the detriment of its foreign relations flexibility and to the encouragement of adversary terrorist groups.

The announcement of a "No boots on the ground policy" was meant to assuage the American public. But its main effects were 1) to inform terrorist groups that they could operate freely with only token air bombardment from America and its allies; 2) to inform allies that America – all of America – was unwilling to engage enemies out of fear of casualties and domestic discord; and 3) to inform major antagonists such as Russia and China that America was not to be feared allowing them to pursue expansionist aggressions.

A reduction in domestic turmoil resulted but at a price to be paid in the future for the foreign enemies they unleashed.

A better policy would have been merely to announce a major air effort to quell ISIS and other terrorist groups and leave open the question of using ground forces. This approach would have unsettled the enemies, gave freedom of action to the American government and encouraged our allies. Yes there would be outcries from domestic sources. But a strong President and Congress with an American public that had confidence in their judgment could have succeeded in muting the criticism of domestic elements and silenced the press who are rather often demanding all the details of government plans for their benefit and incidentally, and unconsciously, for the benefit of enemies. Here we must remember that we are at war, a silent war, and we must remember the World War II slogan, "Loose lips sink ships." The "No boots on the ground policy" announcement sank the ship of intimidation of enemies by the American nation.

An American public with confidence in its elected leaders give those leaders the freedom of action to take steps, or not take steps, keeping enemies in the dark and uncertain. A confused enemy is less of a threat. A knowing enemy can take action against us relying on our own statements restraining ourselves in advance.

Leaders lead, as Harry Truman so admirably showed in the Korean conflict in spite of a war weary public.

4.2 Indecisive American Behavior makes Allies Uneasy and Enemies Adventurist

The allies of the United States look to it for leadership. Sadly the American government in recent years has displayed vacillation and an indecisive foreign policy. It has abandoned friends several times to avoid confrontations with major foes. As a result allies are slow to "come on board" in critical situations and, when they do come on board, often provide only minimal support.

For example, the United States had no clear cut response to the initial Russian seizure of the Crimea from the Ukraine. The subsequent Russian inspired revolt in the Eastern Ukraine led the United States and European allies to impose economic sanctions – to which the Russians could only laugh – the acquisition of a large part of the Ukraine and a port on the Black Sea far outweighed sanctions that could have no lasting effect. The hesitancy of the American government and its weak response filled our new Eastern European allies with dismay. Sending a division of American troops to Poland would have been the appropriate response. Unfortunately, American public opinion looked with favor on the President's tepid actions. The Presidential response like the Munich solution prior to World War II will only lead to further aggression by Russia and China along their borders. We see it in progress now in Central Asia and the East and South China Seas.

The only view that one can take of the American posture is that of reluctant defensiveness that falls short of being effective. The American air response to ISIS illustrates this point.

The trust of America's allies is now at low ebb with an indecisive President unable to posture the Western World for a successful peace and long term security.

4.3 Weak Response to Aggression Leads to Growth in Enemy Power

The United States government has clearly adopted a weak response tactic to aggression by significant potential foes ranging from North Korea and Iran to Russia and China. At the time of this writing the news media are talking of a nuclear deal with Iran. One of course knows the quid pro quo of such a deal – American wealth and technology for Iranian assurances that they will not complete development of nuclear missiles. The problem of this sort of approach is twofold: how long can a financially strapped America buy peace, and how long will such deals last. Our view is simple. The deals will last as long as the adversary can milk America. Blackmail, to which this approach amounts, can never bring long lasting solutions. They can only delay the resumption of hostilities – hostilities with a stronger and bolder adversary.

American allies see American deal making with adversaries as a form of capitulation. Their response is to doubt America's resolve and to hesitate to support American initiatives. Lack of support by allies indirectly strengthens adversaries.

5. Specific Foreign Situations

Currently there are many foreign policy situations facing the United States. In this chapter we will examine some of the more important situations. Fortunately, or more likely unfortunately, some of them will change in the near future for better or worse. Based on the author's theory of history[15] the United States can expect an overall downtrend until about 2050.

5.1 Ebola and Other Epidemics – An International Threat

Presently the world is facing a potential Ebola epidemic. Ebola is largely confined to West Africa at the moment and appears to be diminishing as a world-wide epidemic threat.

Should Ebola have succeeded in becoming a world-wide epidemic then the world's population might have been cut in half from six billion to roughly three billion if the Ebola mortality rate of 50% in West Africa prevailed throughout the world. Since the second and third world populations have health care similar to West Africa their mortality rate would probably have been comparable. If we look back to the Middle Ages and the Black Death plague which had a high mortality rate then we see Europe took a hundred years to recover. We may expect a

---

[15] Blaha (2014c), (2013b) and (2010) as well as earlier books.

longer recovery period (perhaps two hundred years) if a current plague killed half the world's population.

Ebola looks to be ending as a threat. However there are other potential epidemic threats lying in the wings that may perhaps blossom in the near future.

A recent study[16] of diseases that threaten to become epidemics revealed that the number of such disease outbreaks have quadrupled since 1980. These outbreaks are largely due to animal to human disease transmission just as Ebola jumped from bush animals to humans.

The growth in potential epidemics requires a world health care system that can come into play whenever a serious threat emerges. The Ebola fiasco with poor in in-country care, poor response from the international community, and poor response in quarantine containment in the United States suggests that there is a need for a formal United Nations organization to deal with epidemic threats. This organization could stockpile general purpose medical equipment at key locations around the world, and have a database of trained volunteers on call should an epidemic develop.

5.2 Muslim Nation Building

The people of Islam speak of an Islamic Nation although Islam is spread across many countries that often have conflicts with each other. There is also the religious division within Islam between Sunni and Shia Muslims.

To some extent the divisions in the Muslim world are analogous to divisions in the Christian world between nations

---

[16] K. Smith et al, Journal of the Royal Society Interface, DOI: 10.1098/rsif.2014.0950.

and between various Christian denominations such as Eastern Orthodox vs. Western Christendom.

Potentially the nations of Islam could unite into perhaps Sunni and Shia nations or perhaps into several large nations. Given large oil and mineral resources, and a large population, a sizeable Muslim nation would be a formidable competitor for the current leading nations of the world. Iran, which is large but not comparable to a Muslim nation the size of Indonesia, illustrates the potential threat that a sizeable Muslim nation could pose for the West as well as Russia and China. (These nations have restive Muslim minority groups within them.)

The big question is whether a large Muslim nation or empire will appear. Such nations usually are the creation of a charismatic leader such as Napoleon, or the result of an overwhelming victorious army often created by a major event that galvanizes the population into war – jihad. The current worry is that ISIS may be the seed of an empire. Their desire to create a caliphate argues for great ambitions within their leaders and soldiers.[17] We shall see!

5.2.1 The War with ISIS

ISIS first acquired international attention by the rapid conquest of sizeable areas in Iraq and Syria. Their fierce fundamentalism, their bravery, and their ferocious treatment of enemies and captives (public beheadings and other atrocities) excited the attention of the news media. Then their successes in northern Iraq and Syria raised the specter of a snowballing

---

[17] The theory of History presented in Blaha (2010) suggests that Islam will enter a "Universal State" period – an empire – in 2480 AD after 70 years of additional growth in which it is currently, and a subsequent "Time of Troubles" period of 400 years of warring states. The quoted terminology is A. Toynbee's although the specified times are the author's.

fundamentalist organization that might well conquer large parts of Iraq and Syria. Their announced goal of creating a caliphate revealed an ambition to create a Muslim empire. Their success on the battlefield and extremely positive comments in the news media raised concerns that they might succeed in reaching their goals.

The American government, and allied governments, then started taking countermeasures with aerial warfare with a commitment to the American people of "No boots on the ground." President Obama's remarks can be easily understood considering the long, expensive efforts in Iraq that seems to have been for naught. The American people did not want another fruitless venture in Iraq. At this writing the United States government has committed three thousand troops to act as advisors to ISIS opponents. Remembering the beginning stages of the Vietnam War when American advisors started being sent to South Vietnam one can only hope that a gradual engagement of American troops in Iraq does not begin. As noted earlier in this section a major Muslim state is not likely to develop for many centuries. And as we note later a more strategically sensible procedure would be for the West not to enter into internal Muslim conflicts. The West has no true friends in the Muslim world. Western interference would be regarded as "Crusaderism" by all Muslims – even those with which we ally. Thus non-interference by the West is the best policy for the West for the next century or so. The only possible exception is the protection of Israel. However the Israelis have shown themselves to be quite capable of defending themselves.

Should ISIS triumph to an extent that cannot be ignored then concrete action by the West might be justifiable. A world-wide terrorist campaign motivated and encouraged by the success of ISIS, and the universal Muslim hope of a unified Islamic Nation, would be cause for action.

The United States government has indirectly promoted ISIS to a major foe. By identifying to the news media the potential danger of ISIS, the ISIS goal of a caliphate, the spread of ISIS over largely desert areas, the failures of opposing forces, and the growing international support of ISIS – even now in Egypt, and the flow of volunteers to help ISIS; the United States has puffed ISIS up to major league status. Al Qaeda has also begun a more vigorous campaign against the West due to ISIS' stimulation. Yemen is under threat at the time of this writing.

It is now clear that an Islamic surge is underway throughout the Mideast. The gradualist approach of the United States may be mistaken as it gives time to the Muslim terrorist factions to achieve further triumphs, to acquire stockpiled American weaponry, and to inspire the Muslim populace. The United States should give thought to a massive retaliatory attack to humble ISIS. After success a rapid withdrawal should follow. Then repeated, unceasing, air attacks on any enemy troop concentrations should follow – not five attacks a day as the United States and allies are doing now but rather heavy bombardment along the lines of the US strategy in the first Iraqi confrontation. *Thorough, fast, suppression of an Islamic surge is a necessity.*

5.2.2 Let Islam Resolve its own Internal Conflicts!

It is a little known fact of history that the Crusaders that conquered the Holy Land achieved a victory but their methods of conquest and the way that they administered the kingdoms they established caused the still largely Christian population of the Holy Land, Egypt and remainder of the Middle East to convert to Islam *en masse*. The Christian population had not converted during centuries of Islamic rule. The Crusader invasion led to a rapid Islamization of the Christian populace.

The lessons, if there are any, to be learned from this episode of History are that external interference/invasion of Muslim lands does not have lasting effects, and tends to arouse the resident population to enmity. Invasions create enemies.

We are seeing these lessons reflected in the aftermath of the Iraq and Afghanistan wars. Both countries are teetering on the brink of civil war or are in a civil war. Both countries are becoming anti-Western and fundamentalist. The West has some friends in these countries. But they see the way the wind is blowing and will capitulate to the fundamentalists.

What has the tremendous investment of lives and money done for the West? Apparently nothing. The benefits are being blown away by the sands of time and a populace deeply committed to Islam. One cannot win lasting benefits from a war with a strongly religious community. That being the case, the West should consider a posture of total non-interference in Muslim affairs. We should not sacrifice our young people. We should not sacrifice our resources.

Consider the case of Syria where there are three contending Muslim factions: the Assad faction, an opposing fundamentalist group, and now ISIS. All these groups are anti-Western. If any of them is victorious they will be our enemy no matter how much aid we might have given them.

What is the best position for the West to take? Let them resolve their differences by themselves – for we have nothing to gain from helping any faction.

In general, the West should buy their oil as needed and sell them food and weapons at the going world prices. Further, since we have seen Muslim immigrants, turn violent and terrorist in both mind and fact we should sharply limit immigration from these countries. We should provide no technology unless it serves America and/or promotes a cleaner environment. We should not provide military training or advisors to any Muslim country.

Muslim students should be allowed in the United States in the hope that they will benefit from being exposed to the atmosphere of a free country. However, they should be carefully screened, and interviewed yearly by Homeland Security, since some students have engaged in terrorist activities.

The alternative to this approach is American loss of life and treasure fighting conflicts in support of dubious allies with no long term benefit to America. At the time of this writing President Obama appears to be changing course and saying there are circumstances that would lead to sending troops to the Middle East. This softening posture shows the ease with which America can be drawn into widening conflict in the worst possible manner – through gradual involvement that gives an enemy time to gain strength. *Descensus Averni Facile*!

5.2.3 The Failed Strategy of Eliminating Muslim Dictators

In recent years we have seen the demise of several major dictators of Muslim countries: Libya, Egypt, and Iraq. It is possible that President Assad of Syria will also be eliminated if either of the two rebel movements in Syria succeeds.

Have these changes been of benefit to the United States or to the Muslim people of these own countries? The answer is clearly no. The United States lost opposing leaders with which it could possibly negotiate favorable agreements. It now faces a rabble and deep instability in all these countries with the likelihood that Muslim Fundamentalists will eventually take control of these countries with a deeper enmity towards the United States. The result is likely to be more friction, more conflicts, a greater danger to friends such as Israel. Frankly an entrenched dictator is more likely to attend to internal dissension and to protecting his own power. Fundamentalist groups, after achieving power, look to external adventures thinking to promote Islam.

Again the only valid conclusion that these considerations lead to is that the United States should not interfere in Muslim countries as long as they don't significantly present a terrorist or military threat. The oppression of their native populations, while deplorable, cannot be ended by American action. Iraq and Afghanistan, after massive United States efforts, do not have better governments or a happier populace. Rather they have a higher level of fear and violence than they did under the previous dictators.

5.3 A Possible Widening of the Ukraine Civil Struggle to a World War

The Russian government has cautiously started a campaign of expansion that appears to be an attempt to recreate the Russian Empire of the Czars. Its first effort was small – the conquest of the part of Georgia that had a significant Russian population. The conquest was swift and brutal, and not met with a significant western response. The United States simply offered economic aid to the remaining free part of Georgia. Arming the Georgians who are brave and highly motivated might have discouraged Russian adventurism before it led to their Ukrainian aggression.

5.3.1 The Ukraine – The Beginning of Bigger Things?

After a few years the Russian government chose to make a larger territory grab by using Russian separatists within the Ukraine who were Russian armed and had Russian troop support, to capture the Crimea and to take control of cities and towns in the Eastern Ukraine where a large Russian speaking population exists. The Ukrainians have responded by attempting to recapture the Eastern Ukraine (the wealthiest and most industrialized part of the Ukraine). The Russians countered the Ukrainian forces by openly using heavy guns and tanks to support the separatists as well as Russian troops and advisors not wearing Russian uniforms.

Currently Russian columns of troops and tanks are reportedly invading the Ukraine. Their purpose is clear – the recapture of at least the Eastern Ukraine and possibly the entire Ukraine. With a probable 150,000 Russian troops in the Eastern Ukraine the western part of the Ukraine can only play the role of a puppet state at best. The effect of this victory on Poland and the Baltic states will be to force them into a neutralist stance.

The mass Russian invasion in progress is taking place under cover of an aggressive Russian display of power using flights of long range nuclear Russian bomber flights along the American Pacific coast and the Atlantic coast down into the Caribbean and the Gulf of Mexico, requests for refueling bases in South American countries, and the beginning of relations with North Korea and Serbia. These moves push the United States into a defensive posture. The nuclear bomber flights, in particular, can only be interpreted as a veiled threat of nuclear war with the United States should the United States move several divisions of troops into Eastern Europe – the only credible response that the United States could make.

The Russians have also developed a new generation of tactical nuclear weapons and of stealth fighter planes that are believed to be superior to any comparable Western weaponry. They are clearly prepared for a major war or to threaten a major war. The cash-strapped Western governments will have to make major sacrifices to achieve parity with the Russians. The leadership of the United States is being clearly threatened but there is little news coverage and congressional comment. "All the news that's inconsequential" to paraphrase a newspaper.

Economic sanctions have unsettled the Russian ruble but have no tangible effect on the Russian economy considering its massive dollar-based sales of oil and natural gas to Western Europe. A tepid response to a major threat.

Putin is made of sterner stuff.

5.3.2 Russia in Central Asia – Oil and Minerals

In addition to its Ukrainian adventure Russia is making significant efforts to regain control (directly or indirectly) of parts of Central Asia with its vast oil reserves.

These efforts appear to be long term and will probably be based on the creation of puppet governments as the former Soviet Union and preceding imperialist governments have done.

5.3.3 The Arctic

There is a major scramble to secure parts of the Arctic due to the major oil and mineral deposits under the Arctic Ocean. Each of the countries bordering the Arctic Ocean has asserted claims to parts of the Arctic based on their Arctic Ocean seacoast. These countries include Russia, Canada, the United States and Scandinavian countries. Russia has begun exploration and drilling in the Arctic Ocean and appears to be taking an aggressive posture on the parts of the Arctic it claims.

5.3.4 Eastern European Hegemony

The successful conquest of all or part of the Ukraine by Russia and the lack of a strong US response will cause Eastern European countries that were enthusiastic to join NATO to have second thoughts. They can be expected to be at least subdued in their rhetoric and possibly to shift to a neutralist position. If Russia further expands in Eastern Europe, through aggression or the creation of puppet governments, then Eastern Europe will progress to being part of the Russian sphere of influence as it was in Soviet Union times. The effect on the position of the United States, and the progress of democracy, in the world will be disastrous in the long term.

5.4 A Chinese Expansionism

China having acquire great wealth through trade with the United States has now moved from peace with everybody to an aggressive expansionist policy. Having finished its brutal absorption of Tibet, it is now making an attempt to take control of the South and East China Seas with their oil wealth, and to acquire control (directly or indirectly) in oil-rich Central Asian nations. It is also quarreling with India over Kashmir and other Himalayan territory. At the moment it is strangely quiet about its dispute with Russia over their Siberian border. The possibility of collusion between Chinese and Russian expansionism comes to mind – rather like the Hitler-Stalin peace agreement and division of Eastern Europe.

China has a very large, very equipped army and a large air force. It is developing its naval power by building its first aircraft carrier. Aircraft carriers allow a nation to project its power as the United States carriers show. When we remember that Japan threatened an invasion of the West Coast of the United States with four aircraft carriers in World War II we must worry about the development of a similar Chinese capability. The critical battle of Midway removed the Japanese invasion threat by the destruction of most Japanese aircraft carriers. China's development of carriers is clearly a threat for America's future.

How should the United States react to China's new stance? Seeing the tremendous wealth that China has acquired through low tariff trade with the United States in the past twenty years, and seeing the accompanying destruction of US industry by Chinese competition, we have advocated a gradual rise in tariffs based on the differences in labor production costs – not only for China but for all trade partners. This tariff program, which is intended to be gradual so as to not create economic dislocations or a trade war, is described in Blaha (2013b). With this approach the massive accumulation of China's wealth to support its military and territorial ambitions would slowly be brought to a halt and China then could devote its efforts to the betterment of its standard of living and to environmental improvement – not to wealth accumulation by expansion and war.

5.4.1 Central Asian Expansion

China is attempting to create puppet states in nearby, oil-rich Central Asian states. It is supporting domestic communist parties in the countries in order to achieve control. An example is its efforts in neighboring Krygistan. China has a desperate need for more oil and Central Asia with its small population is ripe for infiltration.

5.4.2 South China Sea

As part of China's effort to obtain more oil it is starting to take control of the South China Sea. Other nations with claims in the area are the Philippines, Viet Nam, and Japan. Brushing aside their claims China has started occupying islands in the sea and begun oil drilling efforts. Currently China is building artificial islands in the South China Sea which are, in effect, fortresses or outposts, to assert their ownership of the region. The United States has protested the creation of these artificial islands – but Chinese efforts continue as they realize the United States will not take action against them. The Chinese "Ace in the Hole" is their North Korean "running dog" who they can release at will to start a conflict or to threaten to start a conflict.

The United States with its treaty commitments to the Philippines, South Korea, and Japan should vigorously oppose Chinese economic aggression. China cannot afford to oppose the United States in a decisive way without losing its enormous trade benefits. The United States should leverage this Chinese weakness into demanding a fair resolution of the division of the South China Sea and its resources. The World Court could provide a suitable forum for a just solution.

5.4.3 Indian border/Kashmir

China has brutally absorbed Tibet with its enormous territory and resources. Not satisfied with this success China is seeking to take control of areas that are traditionally part of India. The Indian government, aware of large Chinese forces near the disputed regions is attempting to retain its lands without bloodshed. The United States and the World Court could provide a peaceful resolution of these disputes. Chinese adventurism on almost all of its borders betokens a future that could cause a major war.

5.4.4 Eventually Siberia

Just like Tibet Siberia (or at least a large part of it) is claimed by China. There have been numerous minor confrontations between China, and the Soviet Union and Russia at the Siberian border. These confrontations ended some years ago and an economic zone has developed along the border in which Chinese workers produce Russian goods. One can view the situation as a de facto resolution of the Siberian border dispute.

More ominously it could signal a secret agreement between Russia and China to at least temporarily have peace on the border while each pursues its aggressions elsewhere.

5.5 A Russia-China Non-Aggression Pact Reminiscent of the Pre-World War II German-Russian Pact?

Except at the Siberian border Russia and China have different areas of interest for expansion. Thus each could happily let the other pursue its aggressions.

They also have a common opponent: the United States. If they each should more or less succeed in achieving their expansionist goals, then they could jointly attempt to reduce the United States to a secondary role in the world – effectively a puppet state – or even attempt to conquer the United States militarily.

Then Western Europe, Africa, South and Central America, and Australia would be at their mercy. The Russian Empire would be restored and China could then again claim to be the "Middle Kingdom" – the key nation on earth.

The United States must make every effort – militarily and economically –to prevent the outcome envisioned above. Neither Russia nor China are democratic. Their victory would return the world to despotic empires.

5.6 Mexican Non-Cooperation – Immigration and Drugs

Mexico is superficially a democracy with freedoms similar to those of the United States. However the Mexican people do not speak and live freely without fear – of the government (internal spying, police and military tyranny, and of organized crime (particularly the vicious drug gangs).

The Mexican government is incapable of dealing with the drug gangs or other organized crime elements. It is also unwilling to properly control immigration to the United States because Mexico benefits from immigration through the reduction of its surplus, unemployed population and through the funds remitted back to Mexico by immigrants in the United States. Thus the government only gives token support for border control. Further Mexico allows immigrants from Central America to travel (often via Mexican trains) to the US border and then to take their chances to enter the US. *This complicity alone shows the true stance of the Mexican government on immigration into the US.*

5.6.1 Drug Trade

The drug trade through Mexico has corrupted the people, the government and the army – partly from fear of an implacable foe and partly from bribery. The occasional apparent success of Mexican army efforts to curb the drug trade, and the infrequent capture of drug kingpins should be viewed as what it is – a face saving publicity gesture. A captured drug kingpin is a victim given to the government to support the illusion of a serious effort to fight the drug trade. In section 5.6.3 below we suggest a serious approach to ending the drug trade through Mexico.

5.6.2 Massive Immigration

Mexico is overpopulated. Mexico has serious unemployment and underemployment that keeps the majority of the population in poverty. There is no easy internal Mexican solution to this problem. Immigration to the US is a partial solution by partly relieving the population problem, and by having funds remitted back to Mexico by émigrés'. However these benefits have the negative effect of stimulating population growth in Mexico thus leaving Mexico in the same poor condition over the long term.

Ironically, the large increase of Mexican immigrants in the American southwest and California can be viewed as the "peaceful" return of Mexico to its former territories that were wrested from it by the United States in the 19th century.

The social and economic problems created by this massive immigration make it clear that immigration must be strictly controlled. In Blaha (2013b) we outline a procedure to bring about controlled immigration.

5.6.3 Proposal for an American Response

In the early 20th century the Texas-Mexican border area was plagued with small bandito armies who pillaged and destroyed Texan towns and villages. The most famous of these bands was led by Pancho Villa. The United States sent an army led by General "Black Jack" Pershing who roamed on both sides of the border to destroy these outlaw bands/armies. By fighting on both sides of the border they were able to eliminate the refuges used by the Mexican bandit armies and bring peace to the border.

Today the US has good reason to play a strong role along the Mexican border: drugs and illegal immigrants. Under these circumstances, and mindful of "friendly" relations with Mexico, the United States should take two steps immediately:

1. Build a string of army bases at strategic points along the border moving troops stationed in the southeast US to these new bases. These bases should serve as deployment centers for roving troop units sent to stop the drug trade and apprehend illegal immigrants. This type of exercise is excellent preparation for dealing with terrorist units in foreign countries.
2. Enter into an agreement with Mexico for joint operations on both sides of the border to a distance of fifty miles into the US and fifty miles into Mexico. These large units should be used to completely eradicate drug strongholds and illegal immigrant staging zones. If Mexico does not agree to this plan then the US army should stage forays into Mexico for this purpose (and defeat any corrupt Mexican army opponents.)

It should be noted that the drug trade and the illegal immigrant influx have done more damage to the US and cost lives of young people as well as older adults than any action of the Islamic terrorists in the past twenty-five years. America is ignoring its greatest opponents while dealing with the much lesser Islamic terrorist threat.

In addition to the above proposals Blaha (2013b) proposes specific measures to make illegal immigration into the US unpopular including two year sentences in labor camps for apprehended illegals.[18] The current revolving door approach to dealing with illegal immigrants has clearly failed to discourage the wave of illegals entering the country.

5.7 Central America & Columbia/South America

The problems that these countries present to America are similar to those described for Mexico in section 5.6. The major difference is the absence of a common border. This difference is compensated by the use of air transport, water transport, and easy transport through Mexico.

A possible solution to the drug problem in these regions, which is little more than an undeclared war on America and its children, is to come to an agreement with the nations of this region to help them end the drug trade and the violence it engenders in these countries. The mechanism we propose is to station aircraft carriers on the Atlantic and Pacific sides of this region. The carrier planes could be used to destroy all concentrations of the drug lords – agricultural land, military installations and transport. Then each cooperating nation can send in its troops for cleanup operations.

This approach would respect the national dignity of the region's countries and sharply reduce the drug trade without the use of American soldiers. Continuous bombardment of the drug

---

[18] They can be used to build fences along the border. They should receive no pay but be delivered back to Mexico by bus after two years of hard labor..

gangs would psychologically reduce their vigor and strength just as we observed in the early 1990's Iraq bombardment.[19]

The use of two aircraft carriers (and satellite surveillance) would enable surprise attacks on drug lord bases whether or not the drug lords set up early warning systems.

5.8 The Iranian Conflict

The Iranian efforts to develop a nuclear weapons capability are futile. The United States should allow them to continue to expend their resources on this effort WITH close satellite and spy surveillance of their progress.

When they are near completion of nuclear rocket construction, a massive American-Israeli air bombardment could reduce their rockets and facilities to zero. Iran has no possible response except closing the Straits of Hormuz. This threat can be eliminated by the complete destruction of the Iranian navy and seaports. With so many other sources of oil in the world, and more sources developing, a temporary closure of the Straits would not significantly damage world oil trade. So much for the Iranian problem!

5.9 The North Korean Confrontation

North Korea is clearly ruled by a petulant child with some dangerous toys. It would constitute a problem except for the fact that it is a Chinese puppet state. It dances to the music of Beijing.

---

[19] This effort could be complemented by our proposal for controlled legalization of drugs in the US, and the treatment of addiction as a psycho-medical problem. With government control of drug sales on a doctor prescription basis the tremendous profits of the illegal drug trade would disappear. And, like alcohol in the 1930's, an end of drug prohibition (and drug gang profits) would end the drug gang problem. See Blaha (2013b) for details.

As has been shown by events in recent years it will make noise but the Chinese, mindful of their need for access to the American market, will prevent any serious North Korean adventure. It does permit North Korea to sink a South Korean ship now and then. It does allow small border skirmishes and the arrest of foreign missionaries. These incidents reveal its weakness, and the childish nature of a North Korean leader sorely in need of attention from Western media.

Being under Chinese control North Korea is not a serious threat.

6. A Trend toward a Totalitarian United States?

A large number of Americans feel that the actions of the President and Congress together with surveillance and search activities oriented to the prevention of terrorism and criminal activities are increasingly whittling away the freedoms specified in the Constitution and supported by Supreme Court decisions over the years. Ordinary citizens have their telephone calls, emails, other computer activities, and even their mail subject to scrutiny and possibly legal action. Even verbal comments that were commonly made in the past are subject to possible legal action by the authorities.

There is some justification for the actions of the authorities. We have seen, as discussed earlier, an increasing level of violence and crime in many hitherto sacred areas of society such as the school system. And political leaders and congressmen are subject to frequent threats and sometimes violence. We also have the problem of terrorists and the increasing number of psychologically disturbed individuals and groups.

However a continually increasing "big Brother" response by the government threatens the very principles upon which our country was founded. Abraham Lincoln, in the last of the Lincoln-Douglas debates for the Senate in 1858, made a statement that today at the least would be looked at askance and would lead to governmental legal action in some cases. He said words to the effect: "The Declaration of Independence gives us the *revolutionary right* to amend the Constitution, and to dismember or overthrow the government should circumstances justify it." The savior of national unity was not above calling for revolutionary action if the people so wished it and the government proved unworthy to rule.

We all wish for peace and security in our lives. However this wish must be supported by actions that strike a balance between liberty and protection. One would hope that the President, Congress, and Homeland Security as well as other executive branches of government choose to remember the need for a balanced approach. Absolute security is not a realistic goal but reasonable actions to provide for a secure and peaceful environment are desirable. *A country where the people's speech is hesitant to avoid legal action or arrest is not a country with Freedom of Speech.*

6.1 Recent Presidential Excesses

In the Civil War President Lincoln and Congress enacted laws that denied Seventh Day Adventists and other pacifist religious groups exemption from military service. The Supreme Court overturned these laws and other laws infringing on freedoms granted under the Constitution. Other Presidents and Congresses have also passed laws that were found to be unconstitutional by the Supreme Court.

The hallmark of all these decisions was the acceptance of Supreme Court decisions by the Executive and Legislative branches of the Federal government, as well as by state governments. As Stephen A. Douglas, the "little Giant," said in the Lincoln-Douglas senate contest debates, "I take the decisions of the Supreme Court to be the Law of the land" – a viewpoint with which Lincoln did not disagree.

Today we are faced with an enormous Federal Executive bureaucracy that has a massive number of laws passed by Congress supporting their activities and often granting them broad scope for action. The President can make executive decisions in many situations that go far beyond the original intent of Congress and, on occasion, are unpopular with both Congress and the people. Today, as I write this passage, we are faced precisely with this sort of situation: by executive order the President has pardoned five million illegal aliens going far beyond the intent of Congress and the Constitution to allow the President to pardon small groups of individuals occasionally. There is a public outcry against the President's action. There is the possibility of a lawsuit by Congressmen.

But the more serious issue is the President's claim to take action by executive order whenever he deems it necessary.[20] This claim appears to apply to the power to declare war – a power that has been usurped by Presidents of both parties for about thirty five years starting with the mini-war with Granada.

Congress and large segments of the public are unhappy with the claims of President Obama. In fairness we should remember that almost every President since Lincoln has exceeded the powers of Executive Privilege and many have violated the Constitution. The cumulative effect of these errors has been washed out by the limit on the term of the President. Franklin D. Roosevelt was the only three term President. But events in his term in office, the Depression, World War II and his bad health ending in his death, limited the possibility of

---

[20] It is just this type of seizure of power that led to the fall of the Roman Republic. The Emperor seized the powers of the Roman Senate eventually reducing the Senate to impotence. Is History repeating itself?

Presidential dictatorship. World War II with the threat of German invasion on the East Coast and Japanese invasion on the West Coast caused limitations on free speech to be reasonable and necessary from a constitutional point of view. And these restrictions ended at war's end although the communist menace and the Cold War led to a tacit limitation on the expression of pro-communist and socialist sentiments.

Despite the excesses of past Presidents the balance of powers crafted by our founding fathers, the limitation of the military to serve the country, and the limitation on Presidential terms suggest that Presidential dictatorship will not occur. However major curbs on civil rights could occur through a misguided drive to curb terrorism and lunatic fringe groups. *Freedom requires us to realize that absolute security is neither a desirable or feasible goal at the price of liberty.*

6.2 Totalitarianism and Unpopular Presidents

The growth in the strength of the Executive branch, and the assertions of the current President (Obama), has led Americans to be concerned about Presidential excess. In reality the President, starting with ObamaCare, followed by a weak posture for foreign powers (Russia and China) and a supine effort to reassure the American people that American troops will not be sent abroad – a policy on which he is slowly (currently) changing his position in view of Mideast realities, has alienated the American people. Could he become an "emperor" or dictator? Not likely.

We learn from history that dictators emerge from successful leadership. Thus a President who has lost the confidence of the people has little chance of seizing power.

In the past the general view was anybody could be President because the country was strong and the government "ran itself." This view has changed and the people hope for a leader who will implement change: change for the better in health care and social services, and change for the better in international affairs so that American soldiers will not have to be sacrificed for people and countries that are less than friendly – long term.

It is now clear, as we see in Roman history, unpopular leaders were not a threat to the Roman Republic. Similarly in French history unpopular leaders in the French revolutionary governments did not last long.

The "death" of the Roman Republic was Julius Caesar and of the French Republic Napoleon – leaders of great popularity.

An overwhelmingly great leader can be a danger to a democracy. An unpopular President presents no direct danger to the American Republic.

6.3 Totalitarianism and Popular Presidents

In this section we show that we have been very fortunate in having popular Presidents who might have attempted seizures of power but choose to respect their role under the Constitution.

Presidents Washington and Jefferson were popular Presidents. Their beliefs and ideals based on the Revolutionary War, The Declaration of Independence, and the Constitution, made infringement of the freedoms of the Constitution and seizure of power unthinkable.

President Jackson was also a very popular President – a "peoples President" – and a war hero. Again we saw a man schooled in democracy who would not consider violating constitutional freedoms.

Lincoln was a President popular in the North but besieged by a Civil War that began with serious defeats until

Gettysburg. Then the superior manpower and armaments of the North led to the defeat of the South. Lincoln and Congress passed laws that violated some constitutional freedoms (particularly Freedom of Religion) in the opinion of the Supreme Court. Fortunately the unconstitutional laws ended with the War's end. The Reconstruction of the South, which appears to have violated the Constitution – at least in part, was not challenged in the Supreme Court. The basis of Reconstruction was the assertion that the South rebelled and its conquest by arms justified the Reconstruction laws.

At War's end Lincoln was extremely popular in the North. He proposed a gentle approach to reinstituting government in the South. His assassination ended his program and Congress imposed a harsh Reconstruction program.

Lincoln's views made a serious violation of our freedoms extremely unlikely. As we noted earlier Lincoln said[21] words to the effect: "The Declaration of Independence gives us the *revolutionary right* to amend the Constitution, and to dismember or overthrow the government should circumstances justify it."

In the period after Lincoln the most popular Presidents up to World War I were Presidents Grant and Teddy Roosevelt. Both of these men respected and honored the Constitution.

President Franklin Roosevelt, by helping to raise the country out of the Depression and a potential revolution, and by his leadership in World War II effectively had the powers of a dictator but did not exercise them due to his belief in democracy.

Subsequent to World War II the very popular war hero General MacArthur ran for President. While we must admire his

---

[21] In the last Lincoln-Douglas debate for the Senate in 1858.

service to his country, he appears to have had the psychology of a Caesar as his snub of President Truman suggests. Whether he would have turned to totalitarianism if he had been elected will never be known. But his personality and wartime exploits are the closest approach to the ingredients needed to become a dictator that we have seen in the history of the Republic.

Nixon and Reagan were also very popular due to their successful policies. But neither would have violated the Constitution directly. Nixon's violations of law and his false statements were not threats to Constitutional freedoms but simply minor crimes magnified by the dignity and integrity expected of occupants of his office.

However, the Watergate break-ins – violations of freedom by men hired by politicians – are violations of fundamental freedoms. The fact that they were authorized by men at the highest level of the Executive branch of the government is very disturbing. Even more disturbing is the sad fact that violations of privacy, and freedoms guaranteed by the Constitution, by Federal, state and local agencies continues.

6.4 Protection from illegal Searches and Surveillance

Violations of freedom by eavesdropping on the Internet, and on telephone calls, illegal wire taps and bugs, and reading private emails and postal mail, are becoming more common as a response to the increase in crime, drugs and terrorism threats. In many of these situations court orders should have been obtained. However feeling a need for secrecy, authorities have often refused to obtain the required court orders.

Other methods of surveillance using electronic gadgets in homes and vehicles are also becoming more common. Again, court authorization is required but often not sought.

We are fast reaching the point where Big Brother monitoring of citizens is becoming a reality. In the hands of highly moral, law abiding authorities eavesdropping and surveillance would not constitute a threat to American freedoms. However people in authority are quite human. They err in one direction or another. A significant number of people in authority are corrupt and subject to political and criminal influences. Under these circumstances the acquisition and use of eavesdropping and surveillance is fraught with danger to our democracy and particularly to the future of our democracy as eavesdropping and surveillance tools improve.

Is there any protection for citizens for these privacy violating devices? Apparently not. Various federal, state, and local agencies have almost a free hand to eavesdrop as they wish. And they can escape retribution in the justice system by claiming surveillance of potential criminal or terrorist activity. In court a private citizen faces major expenses when filing a lawsuit while government authorities have their legal fees paid by the taxpayers.

Thus we face an increasingly powerful set of government tools that could be used to slowly erode our freedoms and to eventually lead to a totalitarian America – a trend paved with the best intentions: to fight violence, crime, and terrorism – but a trend that opens the door to a severe decline in American freedom and privacy.

6.5 The Trend towards a Totalitarian United States

If a country starts with a clear freedom-oriented Constitution and then after a time is pressed to restrict the people's freedoms, then the trend is clear. The development of powerful eavesdropping and surveillance gadgets that support the restriction of freedoms, and increasingly dangerous times due to violence and terrorism, solidifies the trend towards totalitarianism. In the present case of the United States we would be a totalitarian state were it not for the restraint and respect for freedom of the current generation of leaders.

Our Founding Fathers, having lived under a measure of totalitarianism, wisely framed a Constitution and laws to protect the people. This work has passed the test of time and we still exist as a free people.

But it is clear that our privacy and freedoms are under attack – for good purposes for the most part. So we find airports invading the privacy of people for fear of terrorism. We find that we must not joke about the wrong things in airports or face criminal charges. We find that we cannot joke about elected officials as we were wont to do for over one hundred and fifty years. We can still say "Kill the Ref!" at sporting events. But any threat of that sort about an elected official – even in jest – is punishable by jail time.

Due to the growth of violence in the schools, students have to be very careful about what they say – even as a careless joke.

The net effect is that the American people are being trained to accept the loss of a significant part of Freedom of Speech – of course, for the "best" of reasons. The result of airport security is to train Americans to march in line and shed clothing in a manner reminiscent of entering Nazi death trains but more politely. It is sad that some of the worst restrictions on freedom result from an attempt to prevent bad events.

The Muslim terrorists that have been attacking America and Americans have succeeded in drastically altering America – restrictions on freedom, vast expenditures, and the growth of fear to a greater degree than we have seen since the Cuban missile crisis in the 1960's.

6.6 President Obama – a Brief Evaluation

President Obama had more or less a "free ride" as President in the first years of his Presidency. The country was in an economic recession but the Administration in combination with the Federal Reserve Bank prevented a depression – at great cost as the country plunged into an unprecedented seventeen trillion dollar debt.

President Obama, fulfilling on campaign pledges and the desires of most of the American people, developed a medical insurance system, called ObamaCare, which promised to ease the insurance burden on the younger population. A management team put together a 20,000 page bill that was passed by Congress. The ObamaCare program was then implemented through complicated computer programming and made available to the public. Unfortunately the ObamaCare program was faulty and also misused by people attempting to join. Net result: frustration and significant failure.

Is the President to blame? Most people thought so. However the error was not entirely the President's. He chose the wrong senior managers to implement ObamaCare because these managers failed to realize the difficulty of the required computer programming. They selected the wrong programming group to implement it. The managers were not directly to blame. But they appear to not have understood the magnitude of the task and to find the "ace" programmers needed to implement it.

Subsequently, after the ObamaCare fiasco, major international problems appeared. The Russians and the Chinese formed the opinion that the President was hesitant or weak, and they proceeded to start the aggressions that we discussed earlier. The Middle East Muslims also sensed the President's, and the American people's, reluctance to expend more lives and treasure in what appears to be a multi-generation internal and external Muslim conflict. In this case they were right and the American response was token air strikes.

What should the President do? Again we discussed this earlier. We can summarize it simply: 1) withdraw from Middle East conflicts and let them resolve their own problems, 2) Help our friends who are willing to fight: the Ukraine, Georgia, the Philippines, and so on, 3) Destroy the Drug Lords at their home bases, 4) "Persuade" Mexico to jointly war on drugs and illegal immigration.

President Obama is clearly a kind and well-meaning man. Like all Presidents he must rise to the occasion should circumstances warrant it.

REFERENCES

Blaha, S. 2002a. *The Rhythms of History: A Universal Theory of Civilizations.* Pingree-Hill Publishing. Auburn, NH.

_____. 2002b. *The Life Cycle of Civilizations.* Pingree-Hill Publishing. Auburn, NH.

_____. 2004a. *A Unified Quantitative Theory Of Civilizations and Societies: 9600 BC - 2100 AD.* Pingree-Hill Publishing. Auburn, NH.

_____. 2004b. *Quantum Big Bang Cosmology: Complex Space-time General Relativity, Quantum Coordinates, Dodecahedral Universe, Inflation, and New Spin 0, ½, 1 & 2 Tachyons & Imagyons.* Pingree-Hill Publishing. Auburn, NH.

_____. 2008. *A Complete Derivation of the Form of the Standard Model With a New Method to Generate Particle Masses: Second Edition.* Pingree-Hill Publishing. Auburn, NH.

_____. 2009a. *Bright Stars, Bright Universe: Advancing Civilization by Colonization Of The Solar System And The Stars Using A Fast Quark Drive.* Pingree-Hill Publishing. Auburn, NH.

_____. 2009b. *To Far Stars and Galaxies: Second Edition of Bright Stars, Bright Universe.* Pingree-Hill Publishing. Auburn, NH.

_____. 2010. *SuperCivilizations: Civilizations as Superorganisms.* McMann-Fisher Publishing, Auburn, NH.

_____, 2011b. *All the Universe! Faster Than Light Tachyon Quark Starships & Particle Accelerators with the LHC as a Prototype Starship Drive Scientific Edition.* Pingree-Hill Publishing, Auburn, NH, 2011.

2 References

_____, 2013a. *Multi-Stage Space Guns, Micro-Pulse Nuclear Rockets, and Faster-Than-Light Quark-Gluon Ion Drive Starships.* Blaha Research, Auburn, NH, 2013.

_____, 2013b. *Starting a Resurgent America: Solutions Destabilized America, Economy, Trade Policy, Social Security, Medicare, Obamacare, Education, Child Care, Immigration, Reviving Industry, Crime, Security, Terrorism, Prisons, Poverty, Unemployment, Media Excesses, Exporting Technology, Pollution, Waste Disposal, Space, Research, and Defense.* Pingree-Hill Publishing, Auburn, NH, 2013.

_____, 2014a. *All the Multiverse! Starships Exploring the Endless Universes of the Cosmos using the Baryonic Force.* Blaha Research, Auburn, NH, 2014.

_____, 2014b. *All the Multiverse! II between Multiverse Universes.* Blaha Research, Auburn, NH, 2014.

_____, 2014c. *The Rises and Falls of Man – Destiny – 3000 AD: New Support for a Superorganism MACRO-THEORY of CIVILIZATIONS From CURRENT WORLD TRENDS and NEW Peruvian, Pre-Mayan, Mayan, Anatolian, and Early Egyptian Data, with a Projection to 3000 AD* (Blaha Research, Auburn, NH, 2014).

Toynbee, A. J. 1961. *A Study of History.* Twelve volumes. Oxford University Press. Oxford, UK, 1934-61.

Toynbee, A. J. and Somervell, D. C. 1987a. *A Study of History Abridgement of Volumes I-VI.* Oxford University Press. Oxford, UK.

_____. 1987b. *A Study of History Abridgement of Volumes VII-X.* Oxford University Press. Oxford, UK.

INDEX

Afghanistan, 2, 10, 35, 44, 46

air war, 4, 11

Athens, 31, 32

Attila the Hun, 21

Balaklava, 8

Battle of Lepanto, 11

black market government, 24

British army, 8

Carthage, 7

Charge of the Light Brigade, 8

China, 2, 3, 12, 15, 18, 26, 31, 35, 37, 41, 49, 50, 51, 52, 61

China Sea, 50, 51

China Seas, 2, 31, 37, 49

Civil War, 2, 10, 59, 62

Congress, 5, 19, 20, 22, 35, 36, 58, 59, 60, 62, 63, 67

Constitution, 13, 58, 59, 60, 62, 63, 64, 65

copycat crimes, 13, 24

crime, 19, 23, 24, 25, 27, 28, 52, 53, 58, 64, 65

Crimea, 8, 37, 46

Crusader invasion, 44

Crusaderism, 12, 42

Depression, 63

District attorneys, 25

Doctors, 23

drug epidemic, 24

drugs, 19, 22, 27, 28, 29, 54, 56, 64, 68

eavesdropping, 64, 65

Ebola, 31, 32, 33, 39, 40

Egypt, 7, 43, 45

environmental degradation, 1, 27

Executive, 19, 59, 60, 61, 64

Franklin Roosevelt, 63

gangs, 17, 24, 25, 52, 53, 56

Georgia, 29, 46, 68

Gibbons, 8, 15

Grant, 63

Great Britain, vii, i, 5, 8, 9

homeless children, 28, 29

immigrants, 6, 12, 17, 20, 21, 26, 33, 44, 53, 54, 55

immigration, 20, 21, 26, 44, 53, 54, 55, 68, 2

interactions, 5

Iran, 1, 2, 13, 37, 41, 56

Iraq, 2, 4, 10, 12, 34, 35, 41, 42, 44, 45, 46, 56

ISIS, 4, 11, 13, 35, 36, 37, 41, 42, 43, 44

Islam, 10, 11, 40, 41, 43, 44, 46

Islamic Nation, 10, 11, 40, 43

Jackson, 62

Japan, 49, 50, 51

Jefferson, 62

Julius Caesar, 62

Kashmir, 49, 51

Krygistan, 50

law enforcement, 19, 20, 21

Lincoln, 20, 26, 58, 59, 60, 62, 63

Lincoln-Douglas debate, 26

Loose lips sinks ships, 14

MacArthur, 63

Maine warship, 14

Medicare, 22, 2

Mexico, 21, 30, 34, 47, 52, 53, 54, 55, 68

muck raking journalists, 15

Napoleon, 34, 41, 62

news media, 13

Nixon, 64

No boots on the ground, 2, 14, 35, 36, 42

North Korea, 1, 2, 13, 37, 47, 57

Obama, 14, 42, 45, 60, 61, 66, 67, 68

ObamaCare, 22, 61, 67

Pancho Villa, 54

Parthian Empire, 6, 7

Philippines, 15, 50, 51, 68

plague, 31, 32, 33, 39

poverty, 2

Puerto Rico, 15

Putin, 48

Reagan, 64

Reconstruction, 63

Remember the Maine, 5, 14, 34

Roman Legions, 6

Rome, 5, 6, 7, 8, 9, 15, 21

Russia, 2, 3, 9, 12, 15, 27, 35, 37, 41, 48, 49, 51, 52, 61

Russian bomber flights, 30, 47

Shia, 12, 40, 41

Siberian border, 49, 51, 52

Social Security, 2

Soviet Union, 1, 9, 10, 48, 49, 51

Spanish Flu, 32

stealth fighter planes, 47

Stephen A. Douglas, 59

Sunni, 12, 40, 41
Supreme Court, 20, 58, 59,
    62
surveillance, 56, 58, 64, 65
Syria, 12, 41, 44, 45
tactical nuclear weapons, 47
Tea Party, 17
technology transfer, 6, 11
Teddy Roosevelt, 2, 63
terrorism, 1, 10, 24, 58, 61,
    64, 65, 66
Tibet, 49, 51
Toynbee, Arnold, 2
Ukraine, 2, 30, 31, 37, 46,
    47, 48, 68

unemployment, 12, 18, 21,
    26, 53
upward mobility, 26
Viet Nam, 50
Vietnamese War, 35
violence, 1, 2, 5, 23, 24, 28,
    29, 46, 56, 58, 65, 66
Washington, 25, 34, 62
Watergate, 64
wire taps, 64
World Court, 51
World War I, 2, 10, 32, 34,
    63
World War II 3, 4, 8, 9, 10,
    14, 25, 34, 36, 37, 49, 52,
    60, 63

About the Author

Stephen Blaha is an internationally known physicist with interests in Science, the Arts, and Technology. He had an Alfred P. Sloan Foundation scholarship in college. He received his Ph.D. in Physics from The Rockefeller University and has served on the faculties of several major universities. He was also a Member of the Technical Staff at Bell Laboratories, a manager at the Boston Globe Newspaper, a Director at Wang Laboratories, and President of Blaha Software Inc. and of Janus Associates Inc. (NH).

Among other achievements he was a co-discoverer of the "r potential" for heavy quark binding developing the first (and still the only demonstrable) non-abelian gauge theory with an "r" potential; first suggested the existence of topological structures in superfluid He-3; first proposed Yang-Mills theories would appear in condensed matter phenomena with non-scalar order parameters; first developed a grammar-based formalism for quantum computers and applied it to elementary particle theories; first developed a new form of quantum field theory without divergences (thus solving a major 60 year old problem that enabled a unified theory of the Standard Model and Quantum Gravity without divergences to be developed); first developed a formulation of complex Special and General Relativity based on analytic continuation from real space-time coordinates to complex coordinates; first developed a generalized non-homogeneous Robertson-Walker metric that enabled a quantum theory of the Big Bang to be developed without singularities at t = 0; first generalized Cauchy's theorem and Gauss' theorem to complex, curved multi-dimensional spaces; received Honorable Mention in the Gravity Research Foundation Essay Competition in 1978; first developed a physically acceptable theory of faster-than-light particles; first showed a universe with three complex spatial dimensions may be icosahedral; first derived a composition of extrema method in the Calculus of Variations; first quantitatively suggested that inflationary periods in the history of the universe were not needed; first proved Gödel's Theorem implies Nature must be quantum; first provided a new alternative to the Higgs Mechanism, and Higgs particles, to generate masses; first showed how to resolve logical paradoxes including Gödel's Undecidability Theorem by developing Operator Logic and Quantum Operator Logic; first developed a quantitative harmonic oscillator-like model of the life cycle, and interactions, of civilizations that is based on energetics (thermodynamics) with equations of the same form as those that describe superorganisms; and first developed an axiomatic derivation of the form of The Standard Model plus a Dark Particles sector from complex space-time coordinates and Asynchronous Logic. Faster than light particles are naturally a result of the Complex Lorentz group embodied in his extended Standard Model.

He has had a major impact on a succession of elementary particle theories: his Ph.D. thesis (1970), and papers, showed that quantum field theory calculations to all orders in ladder approximations could not give scaling deep inelastic electron-nucleon scattering. He later showed the eigenvalue equation for the fine structure constant α in Johnson-Baker-Willey QED had a zero at $\alpha = 1$ not $1/137$ by solving the Schwinger-Dyson equations to all orders in an approximation that agreed with exact results to 8th order in α thus ending interest in this theory. In 1979 at Prof. Ken Johnson's (MIT) suggestion he calculated the proton-neutron mass difference in the MIT bag model and found the result had the wrong sign reducing interest in the bag model. These results all appear in Physical Review papers. In the 2000's he repeatedly pointed out the shortcomings of SuperString theory and showed that The Standard Model's form could be derived from space-time geometry by an extension of space-time to complex-valued coordinates, and of the Lorentz group to the complex Lorentz group (which supports faster than light transformations and particles. This deeper space-time basis shows that the Extended Standard Model developed by Blaha has an origin in geometry and is the true theory of elementary particles.

More recently Blaha has developed a theory of the Multiverse based on a complex Euclidian 16-dimensional space that explains (using the Wheeler-DeWitt equation for quantum gravity generalized to complex-valued space-times) the origin of the Cosmological Constant, the origin for the spatial asymmetry of the Universe, and an understanding of the origin of the newly found Web of Galaxies (that links all the groups of galaxies) in our universe.

He also developed proposals for faster than light starships using quark-gluon ion drives and drives based on particle-antiparticle annihilation. He designed new types of starships, uniships, that could breach the fabric of our universe and enter the multiverse with a view towards travel to other universes. As part of this development of the Multiverse he showed that a 16-dimensional baryonic field could account for the major discrepancies in experimental measurements of G, the gravitational constant. This field enables uniships to escape from our universe. In addition to uniship engine designs he described a coherent baryonic field generator that is analogous to electromagnetic lasers.

In the early 1980's Blaha was also a pioneer in the development of UNIX for financial, scientific and Internet applications: benchmarked UNIX versions showing that block size was critical for UNIX performance, developed financial modeling software, started comparative database benchmarking studies, developed Internet-like UNIX networking (1982) and developed a hybrid shell programming technique (1982) that was a precursor to the PERL programming language. He was also the database manager of the AT&T ten-year future products development database. His work helped lead to commercial UNIX on computers such as Sun Micros, IBM AIX minis, and Apple computers.

In the 1980's he pioneered the development of PC Desktop Publishing on laser printers. and was nominated for three "Awards for Technical Excellence" in 1987 by PC Magazine for PC software products that he designed and developed.

In the past twelve years Dr. Blaha has written over 40 books on a wide range of topics. Some recent major works are: *From Asynchronous Logic to The Standard Model to Superflight to the Stars, All the Universe!,* All the Multiverse!, and *SuperCivilizations: Civilizations as Superorganisms.*

www.ingramcontent.com/pod-product-compliance
Lightning Source LLC
Chambersburg PA
CBHW021345090426
42742CB00008B/754